START YOUR OWN COURIER BUSINESS

Step-By-Step In Just 30 Days

CRAIG WALLIN

**Start Your Own Courier Business
Step-By-Step In Just 30 Days**

Craig Wallin

Copyright © 2020 by Craig Wallin - All rights reserved.

Headstartpublishing.com

Dedication

If you've been downsized, outsourced, grown tired of the rat race or just need more income and a brighter future, this book is for you. If you're ready to take charge and become your own boss, this book is for you.

Since the first edition of this guide was published six years ago, I've heard from hundreds of readers who have started their own profitable local courier businesses. I'm thankful they have shared their stories, because their contributions have made this second edition a bigger, better and more useful guide. Thank you all!

Thanks for buying this guidebook, and may your new courier business thrive and prosper!

Craig Wallin

Table of Contents

Introduction   1

Instant Income, How much can I make? Is this the right business for me? How to use this book.

Day 1   **Best courier services to offer**   7

Who uses couriers? Basic courier routes. Tell prospects what you do.

Day 2   **Naming your new courier business**   14

Sample names. Registering your new business name.

Day 3   **Check out the competition**   17

Detective for a day. What to look for.

Day 4   **Pricing your delivery services**   19

Which is best: hourly or per-mile? How to price extras. How to raise prices and still keep your customers happy.

Day 5   **Choosing the best legal structure for your new business**   22

Solo or L.L.C.? Where to get free forms and advice without hiring an attorney.

Day 6   **Taxes and accounting**   24

What taxes do I pay? 3 best accounting/bookkeeping programs. How to pay for a new van with one key tax deduction. Best free mileage tracker apps for your smartphone.

Day 7	**Setting up your home office**	**29**
	Essential office equipment. Best affordable computers & printers.	
Day 8	**Break day**	**32**
Day 9	**How to license your courier business**	**33**
	How to get an instant E.I.N. from the IRS. Required state and local licenses.	
Day 10	**Show me the money - getting paid**	**34**
	Delivery logs and credit card readers for payments on the go.	
Day 11	**Sample courier business plan**	**37**
Day 12	**Setting goals**	**39**
	Secrets to goal setting success. Setting realistic goals. 80/20 rule. Limiting beliefs. Visualize your success.	
Day 13	**Finding affordable insurance**	**45**
	Coverage you must have. Optimal coverage. Surety bonding.	
Day 14	**Looking good with a logo**	**48**
	5 essentials for a good logo. Where to get a great logo designed for under $50.	
Day 15 -16	**Take a break - you've earned it!**	**50**
Day 17	**Marketing - It's all about you**	**51**
	Free and low-cost marketing ideas that work. Where to get great testimonials. The best free advertising. How to provide great customer service to your customers.	
Day 18	**How to get free publicity for your courier business**	**57**
	How to write a simple press release and where to send it.	

TABLE OF CONTENTS

Day 19 Old-fashioned marketing — 59

Free classified ads. Business cards, rack cards and note pads. Where to get affordable magnetic signs for your vehicle. Referrals. What to do when a prospect calls you. Make money with reminders.

Day 20 Internet marketing — 64

How to set up your new courier website for less than $200. Best affordable website hosting. Let Google help prospects find you at no cost. Free online directories.

Day 21 Search Engine Optimization (SEO) — 70

How to make your business easy to find on the internet. Best keywords to use. Local S.E.O. How to set up an effective Google My Business profile for free. How to get more Google reviews.

Day 22 Using social media to promote your courier business — 74

How to set up a business Facebook page. Facebook vs your own website. Twitter tips. LinkedIn - how to set up a business profile page.

Day 23 Email marketing — 80

How to get a free email newsletter account. 10 tips for a great, effective email newsletter.

Day 24 Break day — 83

Day 25 Choosing the best courier vehicle — 84

New or used? Best small cargo vans. Best large cargo vans. How to make your cargo van last 300,000 miles.

Day 26 Success tips — 88

Top 10 courier success tips. Why you should love complaints.

| Day 27 | Networking | 92 |

How to do it right. Courier associations you can join. Networking with future customers. Networking for shy people.

| Day 28 | Time to grow - Adding employees | 97 |

How do you know when it's time to hire new employees?

| Day 29 | How to find good employees | 99 |

Pre-hiring setup. Background checks. Best job boards to use.

| Day 30 | Employee paperwork | 102 |

Why hire a bookkeeper? How to save on taxes. What to pay your employees.

Resources & Forms 107

Courier terms you need to know. How to add tracking and proof-of-delivery using just your smartphone. Forms: delivery request form & delivery log form. Courier organizations. The "Gig" economy - how to earn instant income as a local courier. 16 national companies that are always hiring local couriers.

Introduction

If you live in California and you need to ship a package to Alabama, UPS or Fedex will get it there for you. But if you need to have a package delivered today to the other side of town, or have a perishable item like flowers or medical lab specimens delivered safely and promptly, a local courier service is your best choice.

United Parcel Service and Fedex are the big fish in the delivery pond, and they are very good at what they do. They have also left plenty of room in the pond for the smaller fish, the local courier/errand services that can be more flexible and responsive than the big fish. Local couriers also do not have the huge overhead of UPS and Fedex, so the profit margins are higher in many instances.

Independent local couriers can provide the services which are in steady demand, but impossible to get from the big services like UPS. Here are just a few examples: Pick up a package at the airport and get it to a specific person by 3 p.m., drop off blueprints and bids to meet bid deadlines, deliver blood samples to the lab across town, deliver sandwiches from the deli to the hungry crew in the IT department, get legal documents to the courthouse before the filing deadline, deliver products for local retailers (even assemble that BBQ on the customer's patio), deliver last-minute building supplies to job sites, and much more.

The list of potential customers is almost endless. Architects, engineers, contractors, government agencies, information technology businesses, printers, media production companies, doctors, medical labs, hospitals, schools, associations, nonprofits, grocers, pharmacies, caterers and restaurants, flower shops, professional service companies, such as accountants, attorneys and real estate firms, busy individuals who don't have time to run errands and home bound individuals such as seniors and those recovering from an accident or illness.

Contrary to what you might think, a recession or economic slowdown can be a perfect time to start a courier service. Here's why: when the economy slows, workers are laid off, and businesses out-source more tasks to keep costs down. As a result, couriers are often even busier than in boom times.

This also happens when the price of fuel rises. Because a courier can make several deliveries at the same time, the cost per delivery can be much less than it would be on a single delivery. Therefore, using a courier service can save an individual or business money during periods of high fuel costs. Most energy experts agree that high fuel prices are here to stay, giving a competitive edge to a fuel-efficient courier service.

A courier service is a perfect "shoestring startup," as it requires no formal training or education, just common sense, organization and the ability to communicate with customers and prospects. Start-up costs are low, as most of us already own the three courier service essentials - a reliable vehicle, a cell phone, and a computer.

According to the U.S. Bureau of Labor Statistics, one third of small businesses are home-based. Join the crowd, and start your courier business at home, where there is no rent to pay or additional utility costs. In addition, you may be able to deduct part of your mortgage payment or rent, and other household expenses, like utilities, at tax time.

It's time to declare your independence and get your share of the American dream with a courier business. If you follow the simple steps in the chapters that follow, you can earn an income as a courier in no time!

INTRODUCTION

> *"If you don't change what you are doing today, all of your tomorrows will look like yesterday."*
>
> JIM ROHN

Instant Income

If you would like to "earn while you learn," you can get a part-time or full-time job as a courier while you start your own courier business. This gives you an instant income and lets you learn valuable lessons firsthand which you can apply to your new business.

The easiest way to find courier jobs is to do a Google search for "courier jobs (my town)" to see what's available. In most areas, you can find both full-time and part-time delivery jobs and those that pay per delivery.

In the "Resources" chapter, you'll find dozens of online apps that are always looking for drivers. Some require just a reliable car, while others require a larger vehicle, like a cargo van.

How Much Can I Make?

The national average rate for independent courier services using a light vehicle–car, truck, or minivan–is around $36 per hour. Working 8 hours a day, that's $288 per day, $1,440 a week or $72,000 yearly working five days per week. Mileage charges and surcharges can easily add 10-20 percent to that, and the occasional 10 or 12-hour days.

In the chapters that follow, you'll learn about the essential start up steps of starting your courier business, from getting a business license to troubleshooting common problems. The material you'll read provides the basic information you need to get going. To dig deeper, the resource chapter will steer you to more in-depth material, such as courier organizations, forums, magazines and suppliers.

Is This The Right Business For You?

With all the uncertainty in the job market, including downsizing, outsourcing, forced early retirement, even being replaced by a robot, (Yes, it's happening more and more!) starting a business can be a lot less scary than it was just a few years ago. The internet has made it a lot easier to start a service business, with online resources for almost all the basic business services available at a reasonable cost.

You must ask yourself if a courier business is right for you. Starting a new business takes a lot of time and personal commitment, and you don't what to waste that on a business that may not be a good fit for your skills or personality.

Before deciding to start your own courier business, it's wise to inspect your personal strengths and weaknesses to see if this business really makes sense for you. If it will involve your spouse or partner, get them involved now.

Are you an energetic person?

Whether you are a part-time courier or full-time, running a business can be challenging. You need to be ready to work occasional long days, work odd hours when necessary, and answer phone calls from customers, service vendors and prospects day or night.

Are you motivated?

You will need to stay motivated after the initial excitement of launching your new courier business wears off and the day-to-day grind sets in. Knowing you're the boss now and earning an independent, growing income will help strengthen your motivation!

Are you organized?

Being able to manage your time well, and all the other aspects of your new business are essential to your profits and your success. You'll find tips and advice in the chapters that follow that will help you get - and stay - organized so you can get more done in less time with less stress.

Are you a people person?

The courier business is all about people, from customers to prospects and others. But if you can handle the occasional cranky customer or day-to-day challenges and keep smiling, you'll do well in this business.

Are you a self-starter?

When you start your own business, it's up to you to make things happen. There is no boss to turn to - it's just you. From scheduling to organizing, you're in charge, and the work won't get done until you dig in and do it! Again, the rewards are great, especially when you hear from an appreciative customer grateful for the service you provide.

> **"If you really want to do something, you'll find a way. If you don't, you'll find an excuse."**
>
> JIM ROHN

How To Use This Book

I'm proud of you! You're doing something that most of us only dream about but never begin - starting your own business. There are many steps that go into starting a business, and it can seem like an impossible task. Where do I start? What should I do first? Who can I turn to for help? Now, with this step-by-step 30 day roadmap, you will have the help you need to start your own successful and profitable courier business.

This 30 day plan will keep you on the right track, with detailed information on how to complete each step, together with action steps for each day, starting at the very beginning. Keep in mind you can do these steps at your own pace. Although each step is a day, if you need more time, just consider these to be steps.

If you finish a day's task and want to get started on the next day's task, go for it! "Make up days" are included if you need to take a break or if you get behind a bit.

Remember, you need to work on this plan at your pace so you feel comfortable, not rushed or pressured to finish. If you work hard and make it all happen in 30 days, congratulations! But if you need to spread this daily plan out over more time, that's okay too.

If you think 30 days is not enough time, just remember Mark Zuckerberg wrote the first version of Facebook in just 30 days! So what are you waiting for? Let's get started.

DAY 1

Courier Services to Offer

Here is a list of businesses and organizations that commonly use couriers and the services they use. When you survey your local business community, you may find even more prospective customers.

- **Accountants & Bookkeepers** often use couriers and errand services to deliver and pick up documents, such as payroll records, tax returns and reports.
- **Architects.** Documents & plans need to be delivered to customers and contractors.
- **Attorneys and Law firms** use couriers to deliver and pick up litigation documents, court filings and rush work. Another related legal area that many couriers find profitable is process serving. Rules vary from state to state, so if you want to explore this niche, talk to a few lawyers in your area to see if there is a need.
- **Banks.** Local banks that provide mortgages and related loans often use couriers to deliver and pick up loan-related documents.
- **Business Parks.** These clusters of small businesses are a good source of work for couriers. Visit any in your area and chat with business owners and managers to let them know you can deliver and pick up documents, parts and products for them.

Caterers & Restaurants. Delivering meals, both hot and cold, can be a profitable niche for a courier/errand service. One local caterer does a thriving business preparing frozen meals for busy customers who like to heat and eat. The courier delivers a week's worth of frozen meals to each customer, using several large Igloo coolers to keep the meals frozen. With over a hundred customers, it's become a large source of revenue for this courier.

Chamber of Commerce. It usually costs from $100 to $300 yearly to become a chamber of commerce member, but you may get a free membership by donating your delivery services to the chamber. Aside from the free membership, you'll benefit by having access to all the local businesses that belong to the chamber. You'll find most of them use a delivery service in their business, either regularly or occasionally, and as a chamber member, you can get to know them all at the meetings.

Computer & Information Technology Businesses. Moving computers, servers, monitors, printers, and other gear is a steady source of work for many courier services. It requires TLC and blankets or boxes to handle delicate electronics, but can be very profitable.

Construction Companies. Local contractors can save money by hiring a courier rather than an expensive electrician, plumber or carpenter to chase parts. When a contractor or sub-contractor needs last-minute supplies to wrap up a project or meet a deadline, make sure you can offer expedited service to help them.

Couriers. After a while, couriers develop specialties, such as legal deliveries or medical deliveries, and when they get a call for a pickup or delivery outside their specialty, they want to refer or sub-contract the work. That's why it is important to maintain good working relationships with other courier services.

Doctors. Delivering medical products and specimens is a very profitable niche for couriers. Some deliveries will be "stat" deliveries–a critical time deadline for most labs and need to be completed in one hour or less.

You may need special training to handle what we call "highly infectious" specimens. Most healthcare professionals use what they call "universal precautions" so every specimen in treated as if it could be highly infectious.

Another consideration is what the medical profession calls "specimen integrity," which means maintaining a constant temperature of the specimen from the time you pick it up until you deliver it. If you don't follow this rule, it could ruin the specimen. Some medical facilities will provide the equipment needed, such as special coolers and biohazard stickers.

Engineering Firms. These professionals often need a courier to deliver plans and engineer documents to building departments, contractors, and job sites.

Flower Shops. Rather than having an employee deliver floral arrangements, many florists prefer to use an independent delivery service.

Gift Shops. When gift baskets or other gifts are delivered, a courier/errand service is often the only choice, as many gift shops only have one person running the shop.

Government Offices. Both government agencies and government contractors use couriers frequently to deliver and pick up documents and meet filing deadlines.

Hospitals. Busy medical professionals just don't have the time to pick up and deliver everything from specimens to medical supplies and equipment. One hospital or clinic can keep a courier very busy.

Medical Labs. While many labs have their own in-house delivery person on a regular route, they often need to get outside help for "stat" pickups or specimens that were not ready in time for the scheduled pickup route.

Mortgage Brokers. Industry standards for electronic signatures have reduced the demand for document delivery, but when documents need to be delivered locally, a local courier service can be faster and more flexible than UPS or Fedex.

Pharmacies. Many patients are homebound and not able to pick up their prescriptions. A local delivery service can help.

Printers. Customers are often too busy to pick up flyers, brochures, newsletters, signs and other printed materials, so printers are happy to work with a local delivery service to keep their customers happy. Professional Service Companies. Companies need help to deliver documents such as bids, proposals, appraisals, reports, mail and product samples.

Real Estate Companies. Real estate firms send a variety of documents by courier and gift baskets and gifts to customers and colleagues.

Retail Stores. Many retailers offer delivery of their merchandise. It's usually faster and cheaper to use a local delivery service, especially for items hard to package or oversize by postal or UPS standards. Some delivery services even offer on-site assembly at a customer's home for items such as BBQs.

Seniors. This is such a huge market for delivery services. Many seniors, and others with medical conditions, are homebound or have mobility problems, and need help with the everyday errands that most of us take for granted.

Example are banking needs, such as making deposits and getting cash, car errands such as taking a car to the car wash or for an oil change, picking up and dropping off dry cleaning, general errands such as dropping off books at the library, or purchasing stamps at the post office, grocery shopping and other personal shopping.

Senior errands/delivery can be a full-time business by itself or a steady supplemental source of income for a local courier service. This would be a great specialty business for someone who doesn't want to park a huge cargo van at their home!

Seniors are the ideal customers. They need delivery/pickup/errand services regularly, and they are "sticky" customers. Once you've served them well and won their trust, you'll have a customer for life!

Basic Courier Routes

Regular daily deliveries - these are the routes that require regular deliveries during the business week from Monday through Friday. Although the work is routine, the income is steady and dependable.

Last-minute deliveries - These jobs may come from your regular customers or a new customer who found your website or did a Google search for local couriers.

Dedicated runs - Often required for legal documents or medical specimens, these deliveries are time sensitive and need to be done ASAP, not as a part of your regular route.

Emergency deliveries - another type of a dedicated run that needs to be picked up and deliveries immediately. If you do an emergency delivery, you will make much more than your regular rate. I list suggested rates for many deliveries in the Day 4 chapter.

Tell Prospects What You Do

Providing a list of services you offer will help generate calls and jobs. Don't worry about being too specific with your list. Just cover the general services you plan to offer and add a line at the end, such as *"Don't see what you're looking for? Call us to discuss your needs."*

DEPENDABLE COURIER SERVICE

What: Documents and any package that will fit in a van.

When: We are ready to go when you call.

How Far: Most of our deliveries are within 50 miles of Anytown, but we can deliver anywhere.

SERVICE OPTIONS

Regular: Pickup and delivery in 4 hours.

Rush: Pickup and delivery in 2 hours.

Stat: Pickup and delivery in 1 hour.

Economy: Pickup and delivery within 24 hours.

What we deliver: Art, documents, dry cleaning, flowers, food, medical specimens, plans, product delivery, prescriptions.

"Don't see what you're looking for? Call us to discuss your needs."

To determine what services are needed in your area, visit or call potential customers. Tell them you plan to start a courier service and want to find out what services they may need.

Here is a short list of questions to ask that will help you determine the best services to offer:

- ✓ Are you using a courier/errand service now?
- ✓ If yes, which service do you use, and are you happy with them? Do they offer all the courier services you want?
- ✓ How frequently do you use or need courier service?
- ✓ How quickly do you need deliveries completed?
- ✓ What courier services would you like to see available?

Don't sell your service on this visit. This is just an information gathering visit. It also allows you to get acquainted with potential future customers, so a future visit to sell your services will be easier. If you're visiting a larger company, ask who is the best person to contact about courier services.

DAY 2

Naming Your Courier Business

This is an important step, so take the time to follow these suggestions and do it right! Start by making a list of several business names that best describe your new courier business. Pick a name that suggests what your company is all about, as that name is the first impression a prospective client will have.

For example, Quality First Courier Service tells a prospect what you do and suggests that your company provides a quality service. Adding the name of your town tells prospects your service area, and making it easier for the search engines, such as Google, to find your website when you set it up. That's super important, as most prospects locate a local business using a web search.

Make a list of names for your courier business. For ideas, do an internet search for "courier service." This should produce a long list of names used by other couriers. Whittle it down to a dozen or less that you like, then ask friends and family what they think of the names on your list.

Next, ask yourself the following questions about the names on your list:

Is the name easy to remember? For example, RoadRunner Couriers.

Does the name connect your business to your community, as in: Lynden Courier Service or Chino Valley Couriers?

Does using your own name appeal to you, as in Angie's Courier Service or Logan's Delivery Service? The drawback to using your own name is that if you ever sell the business, the name may be inappropriate for the new owners.

Another option that can help "brand" your business is to use a slogan in your ads, business cards and other marketing materials. Slogans include:

Nonstop for You
There When You Can't Be
On the Run for You
Consider It Done
The Hurrier Courier
Mission Accomplished
At Your Service
How Fast Do You Need It?

After you've chosen a name, verify that you can use the name. Start by checking to see if you can register the name as a domain name, as you'll need a website containing your company name to help customers and prospects contact you online and learn more about your services. If a domain name is unavailable, try adding the name of your town or area to it and check availability again. For example: NewportCouriers.com

Next, check with your county clerk's office to see if your proposed business name is being used by anyone else. If you plan to use an LLC legal structure, check with your state's corporate filing office or Secretary of State.

Last, do a federal trademark search (free at USPTO.gov) of the name you've chosen to ensure no one else is using the name, or if your use of the name would confuse someone.

Now that you've made sure your chosen business name is available and you can get a matching domain name, it's time to register the name. In most cases, your local county clerk's office will handle this.

DAY 3

Check Out The Competition

Will you have competition in your area? It's important to find out before you start your new courier business, because this knowledge can make the difference between a profitable and successful courier business and one that doesn't have a clear focus and may struggle to succeed.

Contrary to what you may think, competition can be good, as it shows there are plenty of customers who need delivery services.

Other courier businesses - Always remember that all prospects compare businesses, especially service businesses, to find the best one to take care of their needs. It's all about service, and so even if there seems to be a lot of competition in your area, you can learn what level of service they provide and do it better.

There are dozens of ways to do this, from providing a higher level of customer service to providing services others don't offer. We'll explore these options in depth in later chapters. For now, keep in mind competition means new prospects will have many opportunities to "shop" for a new courier/delivery provider, which gives you an opportunity to put your best foot forward.

Next, it's time to learn more about your competitors. The best place to start is on the Internet. Search for "courier service in (your town and state)" and also for your state, "courier services in (your state)."

This will allow you to learn who your local competitors are, and learn from studying the websites of other courier businesses in your state. Here's a short list of what to look for:

What services do they offer? Make a copy of the page on their website that lists them, so you can start thinking about how to offer more or better services.

Does their website have an "About" page that lets prospects know who they will work with, their qualifications and their experience?

Is there a "Common Questions" or "FAQ" page that answers many of the common questions prospects may have?

Are prices listed on their website? Pay attention to prices posted by courier companies in your area, as prices vary substantially from one part of the country to another.

For example, prices are lower in the S.E. states, because of a lower cost of living, while prices are much higher on the west coast where living costs and real estate prices are higher.

After you've found out who else is offering courier services in your area, call a few of them and learn more about what they offer. Ask if they are insured and bonded.

Calling other providers with questions can give you lots of useful information about what you should expect to offer new clients. Once you've set up your new courier business, using the tools in this guide, you'll be able to offer your clients a complete service package that's tailored to their needs and meets or beats the competition.

DAY 4

Pricing Your Services

After you have checked other courier services in your area, you will have a better idea of local rates. Most courier services charge by the hour for one-time deliveries, and by the trip or by the mile for repeat customers, after you have learned how many miles/minutes a repeat trip will take.

Rates vary by region, with cities on the East and West coast higher, and the South, Midwest and rural areas lower. When using a car or minivan, national rates average $36 an hour, or $27 an hour for senior errands. Using a full size van, rates average $42 an hour. Here are the customary surcharges and sample rates:

Rush Service: 10% extra

"Stat" Emergency Service: 25% extra

Extra Weight: 25lbs free, 10 cents per pound over 25lbs

Waiting Time: 5 minutes free, 60 cents per minute over 5

After Hours: Before 8 a.m. and 5 p.m. to 8 p.m. $15 extra

Late Night: Between 8 p.m. and 5 a.m. $30 extra

Weekends or Holidays: $20 extra

You may find it is easier to use an hourly rate to compute charges, but if the pickup or delivery is out of your normal service range, add a mileage surcharge. Some couriers prefer to use a per-mile charge for all trips. The national average courier mileage charge is $1.60 per mile for a car and $2.00 per mile for a van or truck.

How to Price Extras

Besides the other extras listed above, you will need to adjust your prices regularly to allow for inflation, as that affects your costs and your bottom line. Every year, the federal government releases its "CPI" number for the year which reflects the percentage change in consumer prices yearly.

Because this is a widely used factor, almost all business owners know of it, and expect their costs, including your courier bills, to increase roughly in line with the CPI number. So when that number is released every spring, adjust your prices accordingly.

Time is money, and you can't afford to sit around waiting for a package pickup because it wasn't ready to go. You should think about mentioning a wait time surcharge in your pricing based on the hourly rate. For example, if your rate is $36 per hour, and you have to wait 15 minutes, add a quarter-hour surcharge, or $9 to the bill.

Give your customers some slack though and allow up to 5 minutes wait time at no charge. If you don't charge for wait time, customers may take advantage of you, which will directly affect your profits.

Besides the extra weight surcharge, consider charging extra for bulky packages, as they take valuable space in your van that could be used for other packages on your route.

Start charging for a delivery or pickup when you leave your office through the end of the errand. If you start another delivery or pickup after completing one, start your charges when you complete the first one. Some couriers start the meter when they arrive at the customer's business or home. Experience will teach you which method will work best for you.

Your goal is to provide your services at a price which covers the cost of your hourly wages, overhead, and a reasonable profit, and making sure your clients feel they are paying a fair price.

Here's a good way to tell if your prices are too high or too low. If you're overbooked, with a waiting list, your prices are likely too low. If you are having a hard time signing up new clients or getting a few complaints about your prices, your prices are likely too high.

Most clients associate higher prices with higher quality and lower prices with lower quality. Never give away your profits by pricing too low!

The two best ways to increase your prices and your profits are to offer services no one else offers and invest in yourself with continued training to improve your skills and knowledge.

If you do one or both, your clients will pay a premium for your services.

DAY 5

Your Business Structure

Choosing the correct legal framework for your new business is one of the most important decisions you must make in the beginning. That's because it's all about liability. Choose the right form of business and you're protected personally. Choose the wrong one, and you could lose everything.

For example, you may think about a sole proprietorship if you're planning to work alone. Big mistake! The law treats you, as the owner, and the business as the same "person" or legal entity. So if anything goes wrong, or you get sued, they could hold you liable for damages, and your personal possessions, such as your car or your home, could be at risk.

In a nutshell, your choice will establish who is liable for the conduct of your business. If your new business does something wrong, or gets sued, someone has to be responsible. You don't want to be that person!

Fortunately, the law recognizes some forms of business, like an LLC, as a legal entity, just like a person. That means that it protects your personal assets.

Most new small businesses choose the LLC, which stands for "limited liability company," as it's easy to set up (most states have free downloadable forms) and does not require a separate tax return to be filed. You just file an additional form with your yearly tax return. Best of all, because of the recent tax law changes, you'll get a substantial tax break when you file your tax return.

To learn more about choosing the best legal structure for your new home watch business, visit www.nolo.com and click on "legal articles," then "business formation/LLC." Nolo can also help you establish an LLC in any state. If you'd rather do it yourself and save some money, the Secretary of State's office in most states will have free downloadable application forms on their website.

DAY 6

Business Taxes

There are three types of taxes you'll be responsible for as a business owner, employment taxes, income tax and self-employment tax. If you do not have employees, you rarely have to pay employment taxes, but just a self-employment tax.

It's a good idea to visit a tax pro, such as an accountant, to learn just what taxes are due for the legal type of business you plan to start, such as an LLC. They can also advise you what information they will require to help you at tax time, such as a profit-and-loss statement.

To keep accounting costs low, do as much as possible yourself. Today, most accounting software for small businesses has gone online and is called "cloud" software, as it is web-hosted rather than from a program installed on your computer. This allows the software company to update programs regularly to reflect changes in tax laws and other regulations.

A courier business does not need a high-powered, expensive accounting system, but something that is simple enough to be easy to understand and use.

It should also be capable of generating invoices for your clients and reports needed by your accountant or tax professional.

As I write this, there are over a dozen capable accounting software programs suitable for your small business. They all have the basic capabilities covered, so it's up to you to choose the best fit for you. Here are my current favorites:

Fresh Books. This cloud-based accounting program is considered one of the best invoicing solutions available, which is important for any courier business with dozens of clients to bill regularly. It even includes time- tracking, so you can easily add billable time to an invoice. You can also add auto-billing and automatic payment reminders and thank-you notes!

Like most, they offer a free trial period so new users can see if they like the program before spending any money. They base their pricing on the number of clients you bill. Because it is web-based, there are no downloads or installations, and it is compatible with all operating systems as long as you have internet access.

Fresh Books is very easy to use, a big plus for a non-accountant like me (and you?) The setup is simple and quick, and the interface is easy to figure out and logical. Help is available online and by phone. When I called, the wait time was under 2 minutes.

GoDaddy Bookkeeping. This software, formerly called Outright, is more user-friendly than most accounting programs. It's more of a bookkeeping program aimed at small businesses that just need to account for income, expenses and taxes.

The company was started by two guys who worked at Intuit, the parent company of Quickbooks, to offer a simpler solution for small business owners who didn't know much about accounting, but needed to have accurate data for their taxes.

This software is also cloud-based, so there are no downloads, and you can access your account anywhere you have an internet connection, even on your iPad or smartphone. There is a free plan if you just need to track income and expenses, and a paid version which is affordable–currently about $120 per year.

Like all the other cloud accounting programs, you can link your accounts, such as bank accounts, credit cards, Paypal and other payment processing accounts. Then it automatically downloads the information daily.

It can create and send invoices to customers, and has a great built-in timesheet, so you can track billable hours to a specific client and send an invoice based on those hours.

Unlike most of the other online programs, there is no extra charge for additional clients. Whether you have two clients or two hundred, the cost is the same, depending on the service plan you pick. To learn more, visit: https://www.GoDaddy.com/email/online-bookkeeping

Quickbooks Online. Everyone has heard of Quicken, which has been available since the mid-80s, followed by Quickbooks. It is the Big Dog of accounting software and is used by thousands of companies.

Quickbooks Online has a 3-tier pricing plan and a 30-day free trial. The basic "Simple Start" plan includes invoicing and estimates and all the normal accounting features. The "Essentials" plan adds an accounts payable function to track and pay bills. The "Plus" plan allows subscribers to track inventory and generate 1099 forms.

The software is web-hosted, so no downloads or installation is required, and is compatible with Windows and Mac OS X operating systems. Setup is easy and quick and includes several how-to videos. There are a huge number of features available to users, but the less-used ones are kept in the background for regular users.

When you send an invoice to your customers in FreshBooks, GoDaddy bookkeeping and Quicken, your customers can pay instantly by credit card, thanks to built-in payment processing. This means you'll get paid faster, and they don't have to hunt for a stamp and write a check. It's a win-win for both you and your customers.

Another advantage of using accounting/bookkeeping software is that you can set up the billing cycle so you receive a "red flag" reminder when the invoice is unpaid past a certain number of days.

The billing cycle used by most businesses is 30 days, so make it clear to your customers that there is a late fee for past due payments. Most businesses charge a percentage of the unpaid balance, such as 2% per month. If the bill is unpaid 10 days after the due date, the late fee applies.

Tax tip: Don't forget to keep track of your business-related mileage, as it is deductible at tax time. The current rate is around 55 cents per mile, which can add up fast when you're a courier. In fact, it's possible to cover the payments on a new van with just the tax savings from this one deduction!

To keep track of those business miles to take full advantage of the IRS deduction, you need to keep accurate records.

Fortunately, there are many apps that work on your smartphone that can track your mileage so you don't waste time or forget to record trips. Here are a few of the best free apps to do that. Just visit apple.com/ios/app-store or play.google.com/store/apps to download or learn more about each app.

- **Easy Logbook.** This is one of the simplest mileage tracking apps to use. All you do is hit the start button at the beginning of a trip and the stop button at the end, then label the trip. Then enter a trip description and you're done.
- **Everlance.** Has great features for tracking business travel, and is also designed to reduce the battery drawdown. You can even add receipts for gas and other travel-related expenses.
- **Hurdlr.** Created just for small businesses, this app tracks your mileage for tax purposes. It estimates tax deductions and can even send data directly to your accountant or bookkeeper.

Mileguru. A simple yet complete app for tracking mileage and other deductible expenses. When you're ready, just send a report via PDF.

Milewiz. Automatically tracks your mileage, and you can view recent trips and the related expenses, such as gas, tolls or parking fees. It is IRS compliant for generating required tax deduction information and can even store your tax data in the cloud in case you lose your phone.

TrackMyDrive. This automatic mileage tracking app runs in the background on your phone and detects all your drives, then let's you store the information in the cloud. Also generates IRS tax reports.

Like most mileage tracking apps, the first few trips are free, then you need to upgrade. But this app is currently less than $10 per year, so it's quite affordable.

DAY 7

Setting Up Your Home Office

Essential Office Equipment

The 3 essential tools that you will need for your new courier business are a computer, a printer, and a smartphone. Let's look at each one and discover how to get what you need without spending a fortune.

First, you'll need a computer to run your business. Your choices are a desktop or laptop. If you need portability, a laptop is your best choice. But you pay for portability with a smaller keyboard, a higher price and higher repair bills. My preference is a desktop computer because you get more performance for the money than a laptop and lower repair costs. In addition, you get a larger screen and keyboard and better speakers.

A full-size desktop computer is the least expensive to buy and repair and easier to upgrade. A compact desktop model is about half the size of a full-size unit and makes sense if you have limited space. An All-in-One desktop combines the computer and monitor in one package. Although it saves space, the tradeoff is a premium price and higher repair costs.

There are hundreds of choices, but you can buy a top-quality model at a budget price - typically just a few hundred dollars. Consumer Reports tests over hundreds of computers every year and consistently gives high scores to HP, Dell and ACER. The Apple iMac get top scores, but cost more. You can save on the iMac by visiting the Apple store and clicking on "refurbished" at the bottom of the page. I've bought 3 refurbs from them and never had a problem, and the guarantee is the same as a new iMac.

A laptop makes sense if you need portability. Although a smaller size is more portable, the tradeoff is a smaller keyboard. If you're using your laptop a lot, the median sizes with a 14" to 16" screen are best, balancing performance, portability and price.

According to Consumer Reports, ASUS, Microsoft, LG, Dell, Lenovo and HP all have highly rated models under $1,000, all running Windows. Apple laptops score high also, but expect to pay more than windows models.

If you're on a tight budget or just want a simple, no-frills easy-to-use laptop, consider a Chromebook. These affordable laptops use the Google Chrome operating system. They do a fine job with the basic office productivity tasks, like email, word processing, bookkeeping and web browsing. Best of all, you can find a decent model for about half the price of most laptops. Also, the Chrome operating system offers the best built-in security that is updated every day.

You can buy your computer directly from the manufacturer, such as Dell, or shop locally at office supply stores like Staples and Office Depot, or BestBuy. Online merchants such as BestBuy and Amazon show customer ratings for each model, so you can get feedback from other purchasers.

Printers

Shopping for a printer can be a challenge, as the bargain models you'll find at office supply stores and online may seem cheap, but the hidden costs of replacement ink can be sky high. For example, a $99 inkjet printer can cost up to $250 per year for replacement cartridges. That's why it's important to consider the total cost of ownership, not just the purchase price.

Fortunately, several of the major printer manufacturers have developed ink storage systems that can reduce the cost of ink substantially. Brother, Epson and Canon all have models available that slash ink costs. Brother calls their system "Inkvestment tank," Epson the "Eco-tank," and Canon the "Megatank."

The easiest way to reduce printer operating costs is to purchase a black-and-white laser printer. That can cut printing and copying costs as low as a penny a copy and will be just fine for most small business office needs. Be sure to get an All-in-One model that will you to print, copy, scan, and fax. Brother makes several affordable All-in-One models, which is my go-to choice for many years. Best of all, Brother has a lifetime free phone support center if you need help. I've never had to wait over 2 minutes when calling!

If you need a color All-in-One printer, both Brother and Epson have newer designs that feature a refillable internal ink storage tank that can keep print costs down as low as 5 cents for color copies and 1 cent for mono. I'm currently using the Brother MFC-J995DW-XL model, which comes with a 2-year supply of ink. Epson has a similar model, the ET-2750 Ecotank, with a built-in super tank. It also includes a 2-year supply of ink.

Smartphone

A quality smart phone will be the most used tool in your courier business tool kit, as you must stay in touch with customers and service suppliers. You may already have a phone and a contract with one of the national carriers, like Verizon or ATT.

But if you don't, or your contract is coming up for renewal soon, visit NerdWallet.com. They have a great comparison tool to help you find the best plan for your small business. Visit their website and search for "best cell phone plans." You can compare all providers by price and features.

DAY 8

Time Out

Take a day off to appreciate how far you've come in just a short time. You're on the way to success as a new courier business owner.

Use these "time out" days to catch up if you're behind the daily schedule. If you need not do that, it's time to relax. Spend some quality time with family or friends, get some exercise, take a walk, or do nothing. You've earned it!

Take some time today to think about goals for your new courier business. Where do you want to be in a year? Five years?

DAY 9

License your Courier Business

Start with the IRS, as you'll need the "Employer Identification Number," or EIN, when you apply for other licenses, permits, and a bank account. Visit the IRS website at www.irs.gov and enter "Form SS4" in the search window.

Next, you can print the application form or apply online. Applying online is much faster, and you can get your EIN when you've finished filling out the form!

After you have the EIN, apply for a local (city or county) business license. Check with your town or county to find out the specific requirements for licensing your new courier business. If you plan to operate out of your home, it may require a separate license. Most states also have business licensing requirements. The U.S. Small Business Administration has an online list of state business licensing web sites–just click on your state to learn more: www.sba.gov/hotlist/license.html.

Many states also require that you get a commercial driver's license (CDL) if you drive a delivery vehicle. Most states use a weight rating to determine what license they require—over 26,000 GVW requires a CDL, for example. Another requirement involves hazardous materials, such as biohazards, which is transported by many couriers specializing in medical deliveries. Check with your state's department of licensing to find out the specifics in your area.

DAY 10

Show Me The Money

Most of your customers will be regulars who will use your courier service repeatedly. If they are occasional or first-time users, it's best to get paid at the completion of each delivery.

Frequent customers—those who use your courier service often—should be able to pay monthly. To do this, you will need to keep an accurate log of your daily deliveries (one log for each customer), with date, delivery address, a signature and a printed name for each delivery. You can either note the total time/mileage on the delivery log sheet or keep separate track of it for billing.

At the end of the month, send an invoice showing either individual deliveries or a total for the month to the customer. Be sure to include a copy of the delivery log sheet with each invoice.

A simple receipt or invoice book and a rubber stamp with your business information may work when you're getting started. After a while, begin using computer-generated invoices, with software such as Quickbooks. Most courier services use Net 10th payment terms, which means you expect your customer to pay you within 10 days of the invoice date.

It's a good idea to accept credit card payments, as most customers expect that you will. You can set up a merchant account at your bank, but before you do, look into Paypal or Propay. Paypal was originally set up to process payments for Ebay purchases, but has grown to over 100 million customers. There is currently no charge to set up a Paypal account, and once you have it, your customers can use any credit card at Paypal to pay for your services. To learn more, go to: www.paypal.com.

Propay is a popular resource for mobile businesses such as courier service providers, as you can accept and process credit card payments using just a touch-tone or cell phone. It also works on the Internet and even allows you to send an invoice by email to a customer and get paid directly to your Propay account. Propay is a part of Wells Fargo bank, but you can transfer funds from Propay to any bank account. In addition, Propay offers much lower annual fees than most other banks, no monthly fees, and no need to rent or buy a dedicated terminal. To learn more, go to www.propay.com.

If you want a separate payment processing option, Square, the payment processing company whose terminals seem to be at the checkout counter of every restaurant, offers a virtual terminal, so you can take remote payments from your customers. Their "card on file" feature allows you to charge repeat customers like yours regularly, say weekly or monthly, at no extra cost.

I've used PayPal for many years and found them to be great to work with. Big advantage - almost everyone (300 million and growing) has a PayPal account. Your customers don't even need a PayPal account to pay you. It's easy to set up and get started in a day or so, and the rates are very competitive. Another advantage is that the PayPal system syncs with almost all shopping carts and accounting software.

Credit card readers. Both Paypal and Square offer affordable credit card readers with their payment systems. In case you're not familiar with them, a credit card reader is a small device that connects to a smartphone or tablet to process payments through a mobile app. They are also called "credit card swipers."

Be sure you get a Bluetooth credit card reader, as they are much more secure and can process both magnetic stripe and EVM chip payments. Because chip transactions are much more secure, credit card issuers are all issuing them.

Both Paypal and Square have similar fees for payment processing, usually a percentage of the transaction, averaging around 2.7%. Both offer "pay as you go" pricing with no monthly fees.

When you sign up, be sure to get the credit card reader that processes both magnetic strips and chips, even if the cost is a few dollars more. Using a chip reader for transactions can protect your business from fraud and chargebacks.

In many parts of the world, mobile payment apps on a smartphone are becoming the default payment method of choice. In China, for example, cash is becoming obsolete, as everyone has WeChat on their smartphone, and in India, WhatsApp is the payment method of choice. Cash, checks, and credit cards are on the way out.

This is happening in the U.S. too, with dozens of payment options such as Venmo, Apple Pay, Google Pay and Zelle. Venmo, part of PayPal is the leader now, with an app that makes sending and receiving cash almost effortless. If a customer asks if you use Venmo or Apple Pay, the app is just a free download away at the iTunes store.

DAY 11

Do You Need a Business Plan?

Although many business experts insist that a business plan is essential to starting a small business, that's not always true. For every business that fails because of poor planning, there are five that never succeed because of too much planning. As the great Michael Jordan said, "Just do it!"

The secret of a successful courier business is providing the services that people want to buy. A business plan can't tell you that, but real customers can. Instead of wasting a lot of time and energy coming up with a business plan, just start talking to your potential customers to find out what they need and figure out how to give it to them.

Regardless of how much planning you do, it's only a hunch—an educated guess about how well your business will do. The danger is, by spending too much time on planning, you'll have less energy/time/money to try new ideas. The secret is to test your ideas quickly and cheaply, then improve and refine them.

And speaking of cheap & quick, here's a way to do a very simple business plan for your new courier business. If you plan to borrow money from a relative or friend—the most common source of funding for small startup businesses—do an "executive summary" business plan to show them you've done your homework. It should cover just the business plan basics, with an overview of the business, a market analysis with a look at your competition, and an estimate of your first year's sales. It assumes that you will not have employees in the first year. Here's a sample:

RoadRunner Couriers Business Plan

Business Overview: Road Runner Couriers is a new courier service based in Portland, Oregon, specializing in local same-day deliveries in the greater Portland area. Our customers will be local businesses and individuals that need affordable local deliveries of documents and small packages.

Market Analysis: The demand for reliable, affordable delivery services has been growing in the area at a rate of approximately 15% yearly, driven by the growth in e-commerce and local population growth.

Pricing by the major delivery services, such as UPS and Fedex, is high because of the overhead of running a worldwide logistics business, so there is ample room for a local delivery service that can offer more reasonable prices and same-day delivery.

Marketing Strategy: The marketing strategy of Road Runners Couriers is to provide dependable and exceptional delivery services to this target market. This will ensure that the business will have a regular, steady income from repeat customers.

First Year Goal: Based on the size of the local courier service market and the fact that Road Runner Couriers LLC will be a one person business, our sales projection for the first year is $80,000. We plan to build our customer base through direct contact with prospective customers and word-of-mouth referrals from happy customers to continue to grow our service as demand grows.

DAY 12

Setting Goals

Goal setting is at the top of my "must-do" list for business success. Setting goals helps you think about your future and close the gap between where you are now and where you want to be next year or even further into the future.

The key to goal setting success is writing your goals down on paper. Just the act of writing them down makes them seem real and make them part of your new reality. Get started by writing all the goals for your new business as if you were guaranteed to succeed no matter what.

Think about what you really want, no matter how impossible it may seem to you now. Take some time to dream big! Next, list your goals in order of importance and pick your most important goal. Then ask yourself "What one small step can I take to get me closer to that goal." Then do it today, no matter how small it may seem to you. Just getting started is what counts.

"A goal without a plan is just a wish."

Never forget - every goal, large or small, can be achieved by taking tiny steps every day toward that goal. Breaking your goal into smaller steps can build momentum and reduce the pressure of trying to deal with large goals. That's why this guidebook is broken into a daily series of steps that can help you start your new business in just 30 days.

Starting a new business is a large goal, and can seem overwhelming at first glance, but by breaking it down into small daily steps, it becomes much easier and not so overwhelming.

Action Steps

1. Write down what you really want.
2. Write down how you'll get there.
3. Write down your first step towards your most important goal.

> *"Find something you love to do, and you'll never have to work a day in your life."*
>
> GROUCHO MARX

Setting Realistic Goals

If you don't feel you can reach a goal because it seems overwhelming or you doubt your ability to achieve the goal, it's time to break it down to more manageable "mini-goals." Henry Ford once said *"Nothing is particularly hard if you break it down into small jobs."*

For example, if your goal of making $100,000 yearly in 2 years with your new business seems too big, break that goal into smaller goals. Set monthly goals, a 6 month goal, and a 1 year goal that are smaller and easier to achieve.

Deadlines

> *"A goal is a dream with a deadline."*
>
> NAPOLEON HILL

It's important to set deadlines for your goals and the smaller steps to reaching the big goal. For example, say you'll contact 10 potential new customers by October 30th. As you meet your deadlines, you'll build self confidence and strengthen your belief that your goals are within reach.

Action Step:

Write down deadlines for all your goals - large and small.

"Most people underestimate what they can do in one year and underestimate what they can do in ten years."

BILL GATES

Most of us are too optimistic when setting goals and making plans. So it's not uncommon for things to take longer than expected. If that happens, don't quit or give up! Stick with your goal and realize that you WILL get there, even if it takes a while longer than you thought.

The 80/20 Rule

In working toward your goal, you'll find that 20% of your efforts will bring 80% of your progress towards that goal. This rule may not seem logical, but it has proven to hold true across a wide variety of situations and businesses.

So it's important that you find the things that will have the most impact and spend more of your time on them. Here's how to find your personal top 20%:

Make a list of all the things you can think of that could help you achieve your goal. Aim for at least 10 things, 20 is better. Next, ask yourself, "If I could only do one thing on my list, which one will help me the most in reaching my goal?" Now go through the list again and identify the second item that will help you the most. If your list has 10 items, the top 2 gives you your 20%.

Daily Actions

When you work on your goal every day, you'll see progress and help make your goal a reality. By taking small steps every day, you'll feel like your goal is closer and it will empower you to push on.

We all have busy lives, so it's important to set aside enough time each day to work on your goals. Just do what is comfortable at the start, and pledge to stick to it. As you become more at ease with your new daily routine, you can spend more time on it.

> *"You cannot change your destination overnight, but you can change your direction overnight."*
>
> JIM ROHN

If you think you don't have enough time in your day to start a new business, you need to identify the distractions in your life and avoid them or get them under control. Some examples: Turn off your technology alerts! When you need to focus on starting and growing your new business, turn off your email, phone, social media and chat.

Next, stop watching so much television, especially the news. The average person now spends several hours a day watching TV, and you can put that time towards growing a profitable business and a better life. Don't let these distractions control you!

> *"Success is nothing more than a few simple disciplines, practiced every day."*
>
> JIM ROHN

Limiting Beliefs

Limiting beliefs can hold you back and create a false reality that can keep you from succeeding in your new business. The most common limiting belief when you're starting a new business is "It's too difficult" or "I'm not smart enough."

These limiting beliefs can cause you to put things off or quit at the least sign of failure or difficulty. Having these negative thoughts is normal, but never allow them to prevent you from moving forward.

When you have negative thoughts, give yourself permission to let them go. Replace these negative thoughts and limiting beliefs with more positive and empowering ones. Instead of "I can't do this," use "My new business will allow me to have a life I love."

Visualize Your Success

Imagination is one of the most powerful tools for improving your life and increasing your odds of business success. The more you visualize your goals, the more confident you'll become about your ability to reach those goals.

Take a few minutes every morning to visualize your goals and imagine how you will feel when you reach those goals. This will give you confidence and empower you to continue to take the steps necessary to reach your goals.

Action Steps

1. Focus on positive visualization every day that encourages action.
2. Remove negativity from your life and focus on the positive side. Your glass is half-full, not half-empty!
3. Every day, imagine your business is a huge success, and be confident it will be.

> *"For things to change, YOU have to change. For things to get better, YOU have to get better. For things to improve, YOU have to improve. When YOU grow, EVERYTHING in your life grows with you."*
>
> — JIM ROHN

There's so much more to know about goal setting, but that would take a whole book. Fortunately, Brian Tracy has written that book, and if you only read one book on this topic, make it "Focal Point."

Focal Point, by Brian Tracy, teaches you how to focus on what's really important, goal setting, time management and planning to build a better and more profitable business and personal life. It's a must read if you're serious about success! You can get a copy at *Amazon.com.*

DAY 13

Business Insurance

Business insurance provides financial protection and peace of mind for you and your new small business. Yet, over half of all home-based small businesses lack insurance coverage according to the Independent Insurance Agents and Brokers of America. One common reason is confusion over what is and isn't covered by homeowner's policies, renter's policies and vehicle policies.

If you have a small home-based business, as most startups do, you're in good company. After all, Amazon, Apple, Disney, Google, Harley Davidson and Microsoft, to name just a few well-known examples, were started in garages!

But no matter how small your new business is, you definitely need business insurance. You can choose from these three basic types of small business insurance:

1. A rider or endorsement to your homeowner's or renter's policy. Depending on your insurance company, you can get an add-on rider that will expand your insurance coverage to include your business. The cost is usually reasonable.

2. An in-home business policy covers a wide range of events, such as business equipment loss, injury and theft. You must talk to a local insurance agent or broker, as each state has its own rules about required coverage for these policies.

3. Business owner's policy. This comprehensive policy typically includes damage or loss to equipment, liability coverage if a customer is injured, professional liability coverage, loss of business income and often includes coverage when you are driving a personal vehicle for business purposes.

The business owner's policy should provide a basic safety net for most small businesses. In most states you can get liability coverage extensions tailored to your specific business.

Other coverages - It may be necessary to have a business auto policy that covers any vehicles used for business purposes. Just like a personal vehicle policy, it typically covers both liability and physical damage coverage.

If your business has employees, you'll also need worker's compensation insurance, which is available through insurance companies in most states, and through a state insurance fund in Ohio, Washington, Wyoming and North Dakota.

If your state allows coverage by private insurance companies, shop around to find an insurer that has competitive rates and the specific coverage for your type of business.

When possible, use an insurance broker in your area who can get quotes from multiple insurance companies. Insurance brokers can also advise you on which companies have the best reputation for quick and fair claims handling.

Surety Bonding - A surety bond is a type of insurance that guarantees performance of a contract. Some companies you provide courier services to may require a surety bond. In a nutshell, if you don't perform your contract obligations, the surety bond guarantees the performance of the contract.

You'll find that many companies will ask if you're bonded, and in some states, it is also a requirement. If you bid on state or federal contracts, they also require a surety bond. The amount of the bond is specified by your state, so you will need to find out what the minimum is and if it is a state requirement.

To get a bond rate quote, do a Google search for "surety bond in (your state)" The bonding agency can also tell you what the minimum bond amount is for your state.

DAY 14

Looking Good with a Logo

Having a logo is one of the most important new business requirements that can make your business memorable and show customers you're serious about your business. A logo can be simple, like the Target Stores bullseye, or more elaborate.

A well-done logo can help you market your house watch business more effectively, displaying it on business cards, brochures, flyers, your website, and other marketing materials. People remember images more than printed words or talk. Your eye-catching logo can put that image in their mind so they associate the image with you and your business.

Here are a few points to remember about planning your logo:

A logo should be timeless, so you can use it for your business for decades.

A logo should be simple and easy to understand and not confuse people.

Never, ever copy or design a logo similar to another, as it's an invitation to a lawsuit, and just plain lazy and unethical.

Will the logo still make sense as your business expands, adds services and grows?

Is the logo easy to see or read in all sizes, from a magnetic sign on your car to a thumbnail image on your business card?

Today, thanks to the many internet-based sources for logos, you can get a basic logo for just a few dollars. If you're on a very lean budget, visit Fiverr.com and search the site for "logo design."

You can spend as little as $5 at Fiverr, but my suggestion is to get a basic logo from two or three designers there and pick the one you like the best. (Give each one the same instructions about the look and color you want.) You can also have them take the finished logo you pick and make it into a "banner" or "header" for the top of your website.

At Fiverr.com, just enter "logo design" in the search bar to get started. You'll find hundreds to choose from, so I recommend using a "level one" or "level two" seller/designer who has at least 100 five-star reviews. That will narrow the field down and make it easier to find the best ones.

Explain to each logo designer what you want, such as text only, text and images, and the colors you prefer. When you have the 3 finished logo designs, pick your favorite, and add any extras from that designer you may want, like a header for your website using the new logo.

DAY 15 - 16

Take a break - you've earned it

Congratulations! You're halfway to your goal of a profitable, successful courier business. Now it's time to take a break and savor what you've done in just two weeks.

By pausing for a while you'll be able to digest all that you've learned and accomplished in the last two weeks. Take a few minutes to re-read the material about goal-setting covered in day 12. If you haven't yet taken the action steps there, now is a good time to do that.

Also, use these "time out" days to catch up if you're behind the daily schedule. If you need not do that, it's time to relax. Spend some quality time with family or friends, get some exercise, take a walk, or do nothing. You've earned it!

DAY 17

Marketing Your New Courier Business

Without new customers, your courier business will never thrive and make a profit. Marketing is an essential part of starting and growing your new business, and this chapter will give you the tools to find all the customers you want, with very little expense.

Courier business owners today have far more marketing options available to them than just a few years ago. Now, because of the explosive growth of the internet as an advertising medium, many of the most effective marketing tools are free or close to it.

In additional to internet-based marketing, there are also dozens of traditional marketing methods available for any business owner that takes the time to use them. Almost all are free or almost free. From flyers to publicity releases, smart small business owners have been using these proven methods to boost sales and profits for many years, but now, thanks to the internet, your marketing message can reach more people for less money than ever before.

I'll go over dozens of free and low-cost marketing ideas for your new courier business in the next four days. You don't have to use all of them - just experiment with several to see which one's work best for your business. Whether you're launching a new courier business or growing an existing business, free marketing can help you grow that business without spending a lot to do so.

Each day, we'll cover a different marketing topic. The first day, It's All About You, explores personality-based marketing, where you, the owner, are the 'face" of the business and how to make that work for you.

The second day, Publicity Is Free Advertising, covers the best ways to build public awareness of your new business, which translates to increased sales.

The third day, Traditional Marketing, covers traditional marketing methods that still work well in the internet age, especially when combined with the use of the internet, and are free or low cost.

The fourth day, Internet-Based Marketing, covers free and almost free marketing methods available to your business, from free websites to email newsletters.

Until recently, business owners had few options, and had to pay a high price for newspaper and yellow-page ads and printed mailers. Today, if you use a few simple internet-based marketing methods, the cost is close to zero.

The fifth day covers Social Media Marketing, explores your social media options, and gives you the hows and whys of the most widely used social media from Facebook to LinkedIn. Each can help you reach your target audience, the folks who need your house watch services.

The material we'll cover in the next five days is meant to be an idea generator for you, so skim the content, and pick the ideas that interest you. I'm sure you will find the perfect combination of ideas to boost your sales and profits for years to come.

Never forget the Golden Rule of marketing - treat your customers and prospects as you would want to be treated, and they will be loyal customers for life!

It's All About You

We see testimonials everywhere, from celebrity endorsements to local folks praising the peach cobbler at Andy's Diner. That's because they work, and better yet, unlike paid advertising, testimonials are free! If you're just getting started with your courier business, free is good.

The Internet has given your clients the ability to spread the good news about your business to thousands of people overnight. If you learn how to use the web to encourage testimonials from happy clients, you'll be way ahead of most other businesses.

Testimonials have a place in old-fashioned marketing. You can use testimonials in a brochure or flyer to hand out to prospects. There are three common ways to get testimonials:

1. Wait and hope for a client or two to supply an unsolicited testimonial.
2. Ask satisfied clients for their testimonials.
3. Have a "stock" testimonial or two ready for those clients who want to help but are happy to okay something without writing it themselves.

When you ask for testimonials, this happens more often than you might think. A stock testimonial could cover features about your services, how happy a client was with your service, the benefits they received from using your business, and so on.

The possibilities are endless. It helps to have a letter ready asking a few questions from your clients so you'll have an idea what pleased them most. This approach allows you to gather positive feedback right away, and you'll also be able to measure how your clients feel about your business from that feedback.

Another bonus from asking for testimonials is that unhappy clients will also respond, so you'll have an opportunity to correct whatever issue that made them unhappy.

It's important to encourage your clients to spread the word, because that can help you bring in more clients. Here are a few simple ways to do that:

At the end of every email or newsletter you send out, ask your clients for feedback. It doesn't have to be anything fancy, just a simple "How are we doing" or "We appreciate your feedback."

As you gather testimonials, post them on websites such as Citysearch.com or social networks that you use, such as Facebook, which provides "social proof" that can be even more powerful and far-reaching than a printed testimonial. I'll cover this in greater detail, including a list of several websites you can use at no cost, in section five just ahead.

When posting or printing a testimonial, provide as much information as possible - a picture, a first name and a city can dramatically increase the credibility. Be sure you have a client's permission for anything you use in print or online.

Your client's praise, in the form of a testimonial, is the best form of advertising money can't buy, so make it easy for your clients to help you succeed.

The Best Free Advertising

Satisfied clients are a small business "secret weapon," as they are usually repeat/regular clients and they tell their friends about your business, yet your out-of-pocket advertising cost is zero. Word-of-mouth can be your most effective advertising if you provide a service that is so good your clients are loyal for years. Here are two ways to encourage your happy clients to share their enthusiasm about your business:

Always give your clients more than what they expect. Zappo's does it with free shipping and 110% customer service, bakers do it with the "baker's dozen" of an extra roll or pastry. Think about how you might surprise your clients when they choose you to help them with their needs.

Ask for word-of-mouth by asking satisfied clients to refer their friends to you. You can even "bribe" them with a discount or gift if their friend mentions their name when they buy.

Always treat your satisfied clients with loyalty, kindness and consideration (Just like you want to be treated!) The more satisfied clients you have, the more additional satisfied clients you'll gain. Like a snowball rolling downhill, it's a growing circle of boosters that gets bigger every day along with your profits.

A Smile is Still The Best Free Advertising

A simple smile is rarely mentioned in advertising textbooks or classes, but it is one of the most important marketing tools we all possess. A smile forms a powerful human bond and shows you regard a person as a human being, not just another customer or business prospect.

A smile makes a person feel good, and perhaps even feel you are a friend. As you know, folks like to buy from friends. Ask yourself how you felt the last time someone smiled at you. How did it make you feel? I thought so. Remember, smiles are free, requiring only a small amount of energy. Don't forget that a smile works when you're chatting on the phone, as the person on the other end can actually feel the smile.

Business success is all about paying attention to the little details, like a genuine smile. Share yours with every customer and prospect you meet and let it work it's magic for you.

Customer Service

Marketing pros rank customer service right up there in the top three success factors for small business. In these competitive times, running a customer-focused business can make the difference between success and failure. Like most of the ideas in this chapter, customer service costs almost nothing out-of-pocket.

Customer service should be based on the needs of your customers. If you pay attention to their needs and wants, your business will thrive. Your success depends on repeat customers. Never forget that a customer's value is not what they are spending today, but what they might spend over a lifetime as your loyal customer.

Listen to your customers. A happy customer will tell five friends about your business, while an unhappy one may tell ten! One way to ensure there are no unhappy customers is to ask for feedback regularly.

Get a rubber stamp that reads: "How Am I Doing?" and stamp it on every bill you send out, so clients can give you feedback. You can do that on your website too.

Frank Cooper, the author of "The Customer Signs Your Paycheck," has a checklist for business owners called The 10 Commandments of Customer Relations:

- ✓ The customer is never an interruption.
- ✓ Greet every customer with a friendly smile.
- ✓ Call customers by name.
- ✓ Never argue with a customer.
- ✓ Never say "I don't know."
- ✓ The customer pays your wages.
- ✓ State things in a positive way.
- ✓ Brighten every customer's day.
- ✓ Always go the extra mile.

DAY 18

Publicity Is Free Advertising

Use a Free Press Release to Market Your Business

A small business owner can get valuable free publicity for their business by using a tool that's more familiar to larger businesses - a press release. It's easier than you might think, as newspaper editors and reporters are always looking for fresh news in their area. A well-written release that contains a story worth sharing with others is always welcome at the editor's desk.

Your story could be as simple as announcing the opening of your new business or the addition of additional services to your existing business. In most instances, it is unnecessary to hire a professional to write your press release. If it's too "slick," a newspaper editor may not find it as credible as a more "homespun" version. Here's what to include in your press release:

For Immediate Release

Contact: (Your name, phone # and email address)

Date

Headline: Write a descriptive headline that tells your story in two lines or fewer. Always remember that a press release is a news story, not a sales pitch. That's why the first paragraph of your press release needs to answer the five questions every reporter or editor needs to know: Who, what, where, when and why, so they can decide whether to share your story with readers.

Be sure to send the release to the right person. If needed, call the newspaper office and ask who covers the topic of your press release. If you are sending the press release to just a few newspapers, consider a follow-up call to ask if you can answer any questions.

A press release takes just a few minutes to produce, and can give your business the publicity that would cost a fortune if you had to pay for the advertising space. Why not take advantage of this free exposure with your own release?

If you're not comfortable writing your own press release, go to www.Fiverr.com and search for "write a press release" to find dozens of affordable pros to help you.

DAY 19

Traditional Marketing

For many, finding customers is the most challenging part of starting a new business. Don't worry. There are many free and low-cost ways to spread the word about your new courier business, and we'll explore a few of the best here.

Newspaper ads. Most newspapers have a "service directory" or something similar, where you can run a regular classified or display ad for your business at a reduced rate. It's best to keep the ad small, but repeat it regularly once a week is about right. Repetition is the secret to successful advertising. After a few months, readers will remember your ad and look for it when they need your services.

Specialized publications. Every community has specialized publications devoted just to businesses, or seniors—both good target markets for your courier/delivery service. Try to run a small classified or display ad in these as well to let these two important groups know about your services.

Free classifieds. You can place a free classified ad at www.Craigslist.org. Use the region and city-specific sections, so you can get the word out to just those in your target area. Try a general courier service ad, as you may attract others in need of your services, such as busy professionals or businesses.

Business cards. Business cards are an essential sales tool to pass out to everyone who is a prospect for your courier services and to those who may refer customers to you.

For the best selection and pricing on business cards, try www.Vistaprint.com. Vistaprint has hundreds of "stock" designs to choose from, including designs for courier/delivery services. Use both sides of the card. On the front, include your business name & slogan, address and phone, e-mail address and a website address. On the back, list the services you offer, and if you have room, "don't see a service—call and ask."

Rack cards. If you're not familiar with them, rack cards are a 3-1/2 X 8 inch glossy color card designed to fit standard display racks. Rack cards are widely used because they are inexpensive and effective, and the compact size means that prospects are more likely to save them than a flyer. By using both sides and keeping your story "short & sweet,", you can get your message across. Leave them with prospects or at your local Chamber of Commerce office rack. Vistaprint has the same stock designs available for rack cards too, so you can easily match your business card design.

Custom note pads. One of the best ways to keep your name in front of customers and prospects every day is custom note pads. Other forms of marketing materials may get tossed, but people always appreciate and use note pads or scratch pads.

Notepads give you what marketers call "top of the mind awareness." When someone thinks of couriers, they also think of your courier service specifically. Every time they need to make a note, it reminds them of your business. Your customers and prospects will have your name in front of them daily, and when a note gets passed on to someone else, your name is in front of them as well.

In addition, instead of having to remember your contact information when they need a delivery or pickup, it's right there in front of them! Don't skip this powerful marketing tool—pass out three or four pads to each customer and prospect. Here are sources for affordable notepads:

www.notepadsinc.com, www.customprintednotepads.com and www.marcopromotionalproducts.com.

Magnetic signs. You'll be amazed at how much business you will get from customers who saw the sign on your vehicle. Unlike a yellow page ad, there is just a one-time cost of around $60. Vistaprint can also create a custom magnetic sign for you, as can www.magneticsigns.com. If you're looking for a vinyl sign for the rear of your vehicle, try www.fastsigns.com.

Referrals. Attracting new customers through referrals is the most effective way to build your business. Traditional marketing methods, like print advertising or direct mail, may or may not work. Telephone prospecting requires a thick skin to handle the rejection.

Using referrals enables you to find customers who want to meet you because a trusted friend or business associate gave you their name. As your business grows, you create relationships of trust with your customers that will create referral opportunities for you.

The first step is to provide your current customers with exceptional service. The better you meet the needs of your customers, the more likely they are to give you referrals or recommend you to friends or business associates. After all, if you don't care about your customers, why should they care about you?

As you build your business, always have a service mindset—"How can I go the extra mile to help a customer." When you exceed their expectations, they will become loyal customers who will spread the word about you through word of mouth or referrals.

The best time for you to ask for referrals is at the end of your regular meetings with existing customers. If you have satisfied them with your service, mention that most of your new customers come from referrals. Ask your customers if they have friends or business associates that could use your services. When you contact the referral prospects, tell them that (name of your customer) uses your service and suggested that you contact them about using your services.

> *"By recording your dreams and goals on paper, you set in motion the process of becoming the person you most want to be. Put your future in good hands - your own."*
>
> MARK VICTOR HANSEN

What To Do When A Prospect Calls You

Prospect inquiries are the fuel for your new courier business because they turn into paying customers to help grow your business income.

Most of your inquiries will be phone calls from prospects who spotted your ad, found your website, or heard about you from another happy customer.

It's important to make yourself available, so use a cell phone number in your ads, or forward your landline/voicemail to your cell phone when you will be away from the office.

If your phone has caller ID, and you don't recognize the name, introduce yourself professionally. For example: "This is Nicole, with Dependable Courier Service ... May I help you?" Once you have determined the caller is a prospect for your service, try to get their contact information: "May I have your name and number in case we get disconnected?"

If a prospect is still interested, set up an appointment to discuss their courier needs and options.

Follow Up - Prospects often need a reminder that builds on your conversation from the first call. For example, a phone conversation might go like this:

> "It was good speaking with you last Friday, Mr. Smith. I could tell you were looking for the best combination of same day delivery service and reasonable prices, and that's our specialty. Thanks for making time in your schedule to learn about our services. Our schedule is filling up, so I wanted to make sure we can fit you into the schedule."

You can convey the same message with a postcard or letter, but don't email, as most prospects may feel it is too impersonal. A simple follow-up is a time-tested, proven technique for winning new clients, and the cost is next to nothing.

Make Money With Reminders

Your existing customers are like money in the bank. They know you; they trust you and are far more likely to purchase from you than someone who is not yet a client. One of the easiest ways for a business to make money is to contact past customers with a special offer.

For example, send out an e-mail coupon to your client and prospect mailing list every month. The coupon could be for specials, like a 10% discount for a new customer, or a non-specific offer, like 20% off when a customer tries a new service.

Everyone loves to be remembered, so think about sending out birthday cards or personalized reminders. For some ideas, visit www.sendoutcards.com. An old-fashioned handwritten note is still an effective tool. Very few businesses take the time to do this, which makes it even more effective.

For example, drop a thank-you note in the mail to each client two or three times a year. Nothing fancy, just let them know you appreciate them and value their business.

The simple act of communicating regularly is a powerful business builder when practiced often and sincerely. Take a few minutes every week to stay in touch with your customers, and you'll be well rewarded.

DAY 20

Internet Marketing

How To Set Up Your Own Courier Business Website

A simple website is the best way to advertise your courier business. A website is the 21st century version of traditional Yellow Pages advertising, because most prospects expect to find your business, or any other services and products, on the Internet.

If you think putting up a website is expensive, think again. The cost of hosting a website has dropped over the last few years, so today you can get high quality hosting for under $10 a month, with all the bells and whistles that used to be expensive add ons, now included free with hosting.

Today, a website is an essential marketing tool for any business, and even more so for a courier business. A basic, no-frills website can help you find new customers and stay in touch with existing customers.

A website can help you build your courier business in 3 ways:

1. Market your service to new prospects.
2. Educate consumers about your services.
3. Help prospects and current customers contact you.

If you're new to building a website, make a list of what you want to accomplish before building your site. For example, do you want to make it easy for new prospects to learn more about your business before they contact you? You'd be surprised at how many prospects do not understand all the services you provide, so have a page listing your services. An "About" page can be warm and fuzzy, with a picture or two of your family, your dog, or local scenic attractions.

Most basic service business websites include an FAQ page that contains all the frequently asked questions (FAQs) and answers about your services, a contact page with both phone and email contact information, a page listing the services you offer, and, after you have them, testimonials from satisfied customers. It's helpful to visit other courier websites to see what others are doing.

If you are like most new business startups, your advertising/marketing budget is tiny. Why not harness the power of the Internet to build your business, without spending a lot of money, by signing up for website hosting with a company that offers not only affordable hosting services but also free help to create your website?

You may have heard about hosting companies that offer free hosting, but here's why you should only consider paid hosting for your small business website:

1. You can use and control, your own personal or business domain name, such as "dependablecouriers.com". When you have registered your domain name, you own the name which can help your search engine visibility when prospects search for a courier business.

2. Paid web hosting is very affordable, and you will get better tools and resources to help you create and maintain your website.

3. No ads. Free hosting companies may place ads on your website. That's how they make money, even though your website hosting is technically "free."

I'm a big fan of WordPress to build a website. Although it started as a blogging program, WordPress has now become a capable, yet user-friendly site builder that can be customized to meet the needs of almost any service business.

With thousands of free themes and free help from a huge online forum of users, it may be the best way to build an affordable website. In addition, there are thousands of "widgets" and "plugins" that can be added to your website to provide additional features like videos, shopping carts, or customer surveys.

Even if you're not a tech-savvy person, setting up, maintaining and adding to your site is easy enough for most users to do themselves, especially with the detailed free videos detailing how to do just about anything with WordPress.

I use SiteGround for my website hosting, because it's so easy to use, with a free domain name, 1-click automatic WordPress installation, free email accounts, and great customer service by phone, chat or email 24/7. I highly recommend SiteGround for your first website.

Get started by visiting the SiteGround website and clicking the "Get Started" button, then choose the more affordable "StartUp" plan.

Next, register your new domain name, which is the name you chose on Day Two. Take some time with this, as you want a domain name that makes it easy for prospects and customers to find you when searching the internet. Here are a few tips to help you do it right.

- The shorter your domain name, the easier it will be to remember. Aim for two or three words where possible.

- The fewer the characters, the better. The average number of characters in the top websites is just 9. Think Amazon.com

- Pick a name that gives visitors some idea of what they will find at your website or what your business does.

- Don't use numbers in your domain name because they are easy to forget.

- Say the name of your new domain name out loud. The best are easy to say and stick with you. For example, Google, Facebook and YouTube.

- Make a list of domain names you are considering and ask friends and family what they think.

- Having trouble coming up with good names? Search for websites that are in the same business as you. Doing this will also help you rule out names that are already taken.

- Make sure your choice of names is not in use or trademarked by someone else.

- Pick a ".com" extension for your domain name, as it is more trusted by the public than lesser-used extensions like ".biz" or ".info"

For more domain name ideas, search for "domain name generator" online. One of the free services that pops up can generate names you may never have thought of.

To build your website, you can choose WordPress or Weebly. Both website builders are provided free at SiteGround. Weebly is the best choice for first-time users, as its drag-and-drop interface is very easy to use.

Once you've chosen your domain name, you'll be asked to choose your plan. My advice is to stick to a basic plan, as it's affordable and provides everything you need to start up and claim your slice of the Internet.

On their website, and on YouTube, SiteGround.com has dozens of free videos explaining how to set up and manage your website. Just visit YouTube.com and type "SiteGround" in the search bar. If you would rather have professional help to set up your website, visit Fiverr.com and search for "build a website."

Congratulations! You're almost there with your new website. Take the time to watch the videos and add the pages you need to help prospects and customers find your business online. Be sure to add your website address to your other printed materials, such as business cards, flyers, and brochures so your customers can easily find you online.

If you get stuck, or have a question, or need a new theme or plugin, help is just a click away at wordpress.org. WordPress has a very active member forum, where you can get your questions answered at no cost. Just visit the site and click on "support" in the top menu bar. Also, SiteGround has an excellent tech support team, which you can access at their website.

Let Google Help Your Customers Find You

If your business depends on local customers, you'll enjoy a free listing in Google Places. Today, most of your customers are using internet search engines to find local services and businesses instead of the traditional Yellow Pages. So it makes sense to take advantage of these free listings offered by online directories for businesses. The most popular, and currently the largest, of all is Google Places.

You can start by visiting http://places.google.com and clicking on the 'get started now' button under 'Get your business found on Google.' After signing in, or signing up, at no cost, you'll be able to list your business. You can include photos or add photos or a map.

Getting a basic listing is simple, but there are a few ways to help your business appear near the top of the listings if you have any local competitors listed.

First, remember Google values good content, so be sure you fill out your business profile with quality information. Follow their directions for completing the listing to the letter and don't leave any blank spaces.

Next, encourage your customers to leave feedback and positive reviews on any web sites related to your business, such as local directories published by groups like the Chamber of Commerce. You can also ask customers to leave reviews or testimonials on your own website, but be sure they are legitimate and genuine.

Last, if you don't have one yet, your business needs a website, ideally with its own domain name. Having a website will give your business, however small it is, a giant boost in the Google rankings.

As more and more businesses sign up for Google Places, those who have a website will have a better shot at a listing near the top. Almost any web hosting service, such as SiteGround, mentioned earlier, can help you get a domain name and set up a Wordpress site, which ranks well with Google, as Wordpress is easy to index.

Besides Google Places, other major online 'local' directories worth exploring are:

http://bing.com/local

http://listings.local.yahoo.com

http://yelp.com

http://linkedin.com

http://citysearch.com

http://listings.mapquest.com

http://advertise.local.com

http://angieslist.com

DAY 21
S.E.O.

Help Your Customers Find You With Keyword Marketing

Today, nearly everyone goes online to do a bit of research before deciding to purchase. Every year that number grows, so making your business easy to find online is crucial if you want these potential customers to find you. A common term for that is SEO or search engine optimization.

One of the best ways to attract the right prospects is to learn your keywords. The keywords you need to know and use on your website or online directory listing are the words that your potential customers are using to research the Internet.

For example, if you provide courier or delivery services, you likely know a few of your essential keywords, but there are many you will never guess without some professional help. Fortunately for your wallet, you can do this for free.

If you search Google for 'free keyword tool,' you'll find dozens of free online search tools. When you type in the keywords or phrases you want to research, the tool will tell you how many people are searching for those keywords related to your business. Global searches are the number of people searching worldwide, while local searches are those in your country.

Besides showing you how many people are searching using the keyword or phrase you entered, you'll get a list of up to 100 additional related keywords and phrases that you can use, together with the number of searches each month for each keyword.

Once you have this information, you can use the best keywords and phrases in your blog or website. Using the right keywords online helps the search engines do more accurate searches and helps you or your business get found by prospects. Even using keywords in the titles and descriptions of the pictures you put on your website can boost your online visibility.

Make it easy for prospects and returning clients to find you by using relevant keywords in all your online listings, both your own site and in online directories where your business is listed. It's another free way to market your business in the fastest growing marketplace of all - the internet.

Local S.E.O.

Since your new courier business will depend on local customers, you must use location-based keywords, such as "courier your town." The reason local SEO is so important for your business is because almost half of all Google searches are searching for a local business. Plus, the fastest growing search term on Google is "near me" as in "Italian restaurant near me." Since Google and other search engines can easily determine your approximate location, this enables them to deliver the results you are searching for with high accuracy.

To make it even easier for you to find what you're looking for, Google provides a "Map Pack," a set of 3 high ranking local businesses, complete with a map of their locations from Google maps. Underneath the Map Pack, you'll find the rest of the results for your search.

How to find the best keywords for local S.E.O.

Do a Google search for words and phrases that relate to your business, one at a time, and make a list of them. For example, "courier near me," courier my town," package delivery near me," "delivery service my town."

When you enter your search term, you'll see a list of additional search terms. Take a close look at those to see if any are suitable for your business. Save your list of search terms to use when setting up your "Google My Business" profile.

How to Set Up Your "Google My Business" Profile

Google My Business (www.google.com/business) is the number one factor Google uses to rank your business in local searches. When setting up your profile, be sure to include your full business name, address, and phone number (NAP). Google uses this information to ensure that your business is legitimate. Also, the NAP on your website should be an exact match for your Google My Business listing.

If it's not a match, Google may rank your business lower in local searches. Even spelling counts here - if your business address is 123 Lincoln Avenue, makes sure it's "Avenue" and not "Ave." so the Google search engine doesn't get confused.

When filling out your profile on GMB, choose a broad category that best describes your business - "courier" for example. You can then choose sub-categories, such as "delivery service" or "package delivery." Also fill out the "services" tab in your profile that describes what your business does.

Google Reviews

Reviews are another major ranking factor in the Google ranking system. You may have noticed that business with many reviews, especially positive reviews, always ranks higher than those with no reviews. So you'll want to get as many positive reviews as you can as soon as you can.

When you get a review, good, bad or lukewarm, reply to it inside the Google My Business dashboard. That shows you care and is also a factor in Google rankings. It doesn't have to be a long reply to be effective. For example, "Thanks for the 5-star review. We really appreciate your business," or "We're sorry your package was delayed and promise we'll do better next time. Thanks for the feedback."

How to Get More Google Reviews

Keep in mind that most customers won't bother to leave a review, even if they love your service, unless asked. It's easy to do. In fact, Google makes it easy for both you and your customers.

Go to your GMB account dashboard and locate the "get more reviews" card. There, you can get a link to your review page that you can copy and paste into an email to send to your customers.

Apply all these simple SEO tips, and soon your new business will show up on page 1 of Google search results. All without having to spend any money. Don't put this off any longer than necessary, as it's one of the best "free lunches" you'll ever receive!

DAY 22

Social Media Marketing

Facebook

Facebook is the largest social media network in the world, with over 2 billion active users. Most users are between the ages of 25 and 65, but the over-65 users are the fastest growing group! That's great news, as these are the people you want to reach about your courier business.

Because of its size and the large number of users, Facebook is the best social media to get your new business shared and discovered by both new prospects and your current clients. That's why it is often called "the largest word-of-mouth marketing resource on the planet."

Facebook can also be the biggest time-waster if you let, as it's easy to linger there for hours. But you have a business to build and grow, so let's focus on doing just that, with some help from Facebook, in less than 15 minutes a day.

First rule - don't waste your money on Facebook ads. No one visits Facebook to look for services or products. They visit to see what their friends are doing. With that in mind, here's how to get started without spending a dime.

It's important to note that you must create a Facebook page, not a personal profile, also called a Personal Timeline. They do not permit personal profiles for commercial use, so if you are already a Facebook user, you must create a separate page for your courier business.

You can create a Facebook Page by searching "create a page" in the searcher at the top of the page, or by clicking the "create a page" button at the top of any Facebook page.

Before you create your new Facebook page, spend some time thinking about the page name you will use. Ideally, it should be short, easy to remember, promise a benefit, and describe your business. A good example would be (if your courier business is in Tampa) @tampacourier.

In the "About" section of your new Facebook Page, include as much information about your business as possible, so current clients and prospects can find all your important information in one page.

You can also optimize your page by choosing one of the pre-made templates. The Professional Services template is a good fit for most courier businesses. You'll find the templates under: Settings>Edit Page.

Next, create an eye-catching cover photo for your Facebook page. Look at other courier businesses, both on Facebook and by doing a web search for "courier business" or "parcel delivery business" to see what others have done.

Ideally, your cover photo should communicate what your courier business is all about, so take the time to do it right. The easiest way to get a good cover photo designed is to hire a designer at Fiverr.com.

It will cost you around $5 to $15, but it's money well spent. Just enter "design Facebook cover" in the Fiverr.com search bar to locate dozens of capable designers. Be sure to mention that you want the image size to be 820 X 312 pixels per Facebook guidelines.

When you've uploaded your new cover photo, click it to add a text description. Describe your courier business in a positive way and, if possible, encourage viewers to click on the cover photo to get more "likes."

You'll also want to add a Facebook profile photo in a 180 x 180 pixel size. Remember, this profile photo appears in a follower's news feeds, in comment replies, and all over Facebook, so use a great photo. (Don't forget to smile!)

Once you've set up your Facebook page, stay active with regular posts. Most pros find 3X a week works well, yet doesn't require a lot of time.

Don't forget to post about special experiences you've had with clients that others might enjoy. Share the story and a picture or two of you and your client in a post.

Is a Facebook Page Better Than a Web Site?

Yes, and no. You can set up a Facebook page in about an hour and it's free. That page allows you to stay in touch with clients and prospects and build relationships. If a Facebook page is not working for you delete it or ignore it. Keeping your Facebook page up to date with your current information, such as rates and services offered, is quick and easy.

But - you are not in control. Facebook is in control, and can change or restrict what you can do there overnight. In addition, anyone can post negative comments or complaints on your page if they wish.

If you create a website, you're in control. You own it. You get to decide what it looks like and what it contains. You can have hundreds of pages/posts or just a simple one-pager.

Consumers today expect a business to have a website. They trust a business more when they see a "real" website. Also, having your own website allows you to post all your service information at the site, like the services you provide, monthly specials, testimonials and more.

My choice would be to have both a Facebook page and a website. You have the best of both worlds - and you don't have to say "follow me on Facebook."

Twitter

Twitter can be a powerful social media tool for your courier business that can help you educate clients about your services, reach new prospects for your business and connect you to other Twitter users with similar interests.

Here are just two of the many ways Twitter can help your courier business:

1. Drive traffic to your website. Unlike other social media, you can reuse content from your website or other original material repeatedly. Your tweets can include your website URL, text, images, even a video.

2. Google indexes your twitter bio and tweets, which helps you get found by search engines. Make sure your bio contains the keywords you want Google to find and index, such as your business name and what your business does. Be sure to tweet regularly so you increase the odds of ranking higher in Google Search.

3. Last, use hashtags (#) to get more attention for your tweets, show your support and help people who don't know you to follow you. To learn what topics are hot or trending up right now, check Twitter Trends or hashtagify.me.

It's free and easy to make an account - just visit twitter.com, enter your name, phone and email address and create a password for your new account. After you've signed up, you can add more information for your account.

Next it's time to pick your Twitter "handle," which is the same as a username. The best handle is your business name, if it is available. You can check all the social networks for name availability at knowem.com.

If your handle/name is not available, you can add HQ to your company name, add a "get" in front of your name, or add your location, such as your town's name, to your handle.

Whatever handle you choose, make sure it is as short as possible, because you only have 280 characters to use, and they count your username in that 280 words when someone responds to your messages.

LinkedIn

LinkedIn is a place for companies and individuals to connect on a professional, not personal, level. Unlike other social media sites, folks who join LinkedIn are not joining for enjoyment and fun but to access new business opportunities and connections.

As the owner of a small business, you can use LinkedIn to connect to other courier services, promote your own courier business and build relationships with other professionals that have common interests.

Getting started is no more difficult than at other social networks. You start by creating your own personal account and profile. A LinkedIn profile is much more professional You won't find funny cat videos or cute baby photos.

So keep that in mind when creating your profile. In your profile, be sure to include your best work-related qualities so others will see the advantages of working with you.

Although you can upgrade to several higher levels of paid subscriptions, the basic account should be fine for almost all courier businesses. Your basic profile can include a summary of yourself, contact information, links to your blog or website or other social media pages, like Facebook, and what you're doing now professionally.

Promote your special focus - for example, if your specialty is same day small package delivery, add a brief description of your last 2 or 3 projects so a prospect can view them. Be sure to add a high-quality photo of yourself, as people are much more at ease connecting to someone with a photo.

Once you've completed your personal profile and published it, you can:

1. Look for connections - people you know or would like to know.
2. Join a group of other users who share common interests.
3. Have an online "business card" where potential clients can learn about and connect with you.
4. Boost your online reputation as a courier professional.

There are hundreds of other social media sites, as you may have noticed when you visited knowem.com. but most are useful only for entertainment, not helping you grow your courier business. These three, Facebook, Twitter and LinkedIn will help you stay connected, expand your network, and increase your profits.

DAY 23

Email Marketing

Stay in Touch with a Free Newsletter

One of the best and least expensive ways to stay in touch with your clients and potential clients is by sending them an e-mail newsletter. By using an email, the big expenses of a traditional newsletter, printing and postage, are eliminated. Your newsletter should do two things:

1. Pass along useful information your customers are happy to read, even forward to their friends.

2. Increase your profits by either helping sell more of your services or attract more prospects who will buy from you.

3. The easiest way to make sure your newsletter accomplishes those two goals is to just ask your clients and prospects what they want before you send out the first issue and keep asking them what they want in the newsletter. How often should a newsletter be sent to clients? Most experts say it's not how often that matters, but the quality of the content. Some prefer a frequent schedule, such as every two weeks or once a month, while others may only do a quarterly newsletter. If you have built a list of loyal clients, they don't really care how often they receive an issue.

Be sure to ask a favor at the end of each newsletter: *"If you've enjoyed this newsletter, please forward it to your friends."* Doing so will grow your subscriber list and your profits over time.

When your e-mail list has grown beyond a few subscribers, it's time to get some professional help. My favorites are www.MailChimp.com and www.mailerlite.com

At Mail Chimp, for free, you'll have access to professionally designed message templates and sign-up forms, and up to 2,000 customers or 12,000 emails a month and compliance with all anti-spam regulations.

You'll love the free service, plus the freedom from tedious mailing list maintenance. Another excellent provider with free service for up to 1,000 subscribers is mailerlite.com.

Ten Tips for a Successful E-Mail Newsletter

According to the e-mail pros, a well-done e-mail newsletter can produce $40 in profits for every dollar you spend. That's a powerful incentive to spend the time on staying in touch with your customers and prospects with e-mails. Here are ten tips that will help you make more money and build customer loyalty with your own e-mail newsletter.

1. Current content. Be sure to date each newsletter issue when you send it out so readers will know the content is current.

2. You don't have to be a writer to produce an e-mail newsletter that gets results. Just write as you speak and focus on the topic you want to communicate with your clients.

3. Your newsletter need not look professional to succeed. Just a simple text message will work just fine. That said, most of the professional e-mail list management services, like www.MailerLite.com.com and www.MailChimp.com offer free HTML templates that can dress up your message.

4. The best ideas for content in your e-mail newsletter will come from your readers. Ask them often about what they would like to see covered in future issues.

5. Keep your newsletter short. If you have several ideas to share, break them up into individual newsletter issues, or include an excerpt, with a link to the full text at your web site or blog.

6. Try not to go too long between issues - two weeks to a month is a reasonable interval to aim for.

7. The cyber-gremlins will always try to mess with your e-mails, so get used to it. E-mails get lost, trapped in reader's spam filters, or just plain disappear. Subscribers will forget they subscribed and accuse you of spamming them, or click the spam button instead of unsubscribing. Just view it all as a part of your learning curve, and stay calm. Using one of the services mentioned in #3 can help minimize problems, and the cost is reasonable. In fact, as I write this, Mail Chimp and MailerLite offer a free service if you have a small (under 2,000 subscribers) list.

8. Keep your sales pitches under control. While folks expect you to sell them something, they get upset if it occurs with every newsletter issue. Experts say a ratio of 80 percent informational content to 20 percent sales information is about right.

9. Stay on topic. Your readers gave you their e-mail address so they could learn more about topics related to getting packages from point A to point B affordably, and other related topics. Stay away from personal topics, as some will enjoy learning about your personal life, but an equal amount will not care, and be inclined to hit the spam button or unsubscribe.

10. Also, post your newsletters on your website or blog so readers can find them at a later date. In addition, the search engines will spot and index them, and help steer new prospects to your site.

DAY 24

Take a Break Today

You've come a long way in just three weeks, so it's time to take a day to pause and do something totally unrelated to your new courier business.

DAY 25

Choosing a Vehicle

To start your courier business, you will need a reliable vehicle. If you are located in a large city with traffic congestion and parking issues, you may want a smaller vehicle like a mini cargo van.

A minivan may be the perfect choice if your deliveries don't include many large items. In addition, a smaller van is less costly to buy and has lower costs for fuel and maintenance.

If you need more cargo space for your typical deliveries, a full-size cargo van makes sense and you'll likely make more money with it as you can haul more packages.

To keep your monthly payments low, consider leasing a van or buying a low mileage used van. For most popular vans, you can find a suitable used van with low mileage for about half the cost of a new van.

Whether you buy a new or used van, remember that you can deduct all your business mileage when you file your annual tax return. The current deduction is around 55 cents per mile, so the mileage deduction can save the average courier thousands of dollars yearly. In fact, the mileage deduction alone can often cover the monthly payments for your van, new or used.

Let's take a closer look at the best vans for courier work. Small cargo vans are more affordable and they have better fuel economy and lower maintenance costs. If your route is city based, the smaller cargo vans will fit easily into standard parking spaces - a big plus in areas where on-street parking is in short supply.

Small Cargo Vans

The Nissan NV200 is the smallest compact cargo van currently available, with 123 cubic feet of cargo space and an economical engine that averages 24 MPG in the city, the best in this size range. if you buy new, the 100,000 mile warranty is a big plus.

You'll find lots of used Nissan NV200s available. From 2013 to 2018, Chevrolet also sold this van as the Chevrolet "City Express.," so if you're looking for a used van, be sure to look for both name-plates.

Ford's popular Transit Connect is the second smallest van, with a 129 cubic foot cargo capacity and a choice of 2 engines. As with most vans, there is a generous supply of used Transit Connect choices on the market, with prices averaging half-off the new price for a five-year-old van with low mileage.

The Ram ProMaster City has 132 cubic feet of cargo room and a higher payload of 1800 pounds. Mileage is average for this class, with its 2.4 engine rated at 21 MPG city.

If your route is primarily in urban areas, keep in mind this van is more than a foot longer than the Ford and Nissan vans, with a larger turning radius, so it may not be the best choice in congested urban areas.

Large Cargo Vans

The Nissan NV is based on the Nissan Titan pickup platform and has a rear-wheel drive, which could be a disadvantage in snowy conditions. Payload is 3300 pounds, and the NV 2500 and NV 3500 models have a cargo capacity of 323 cubic feet with the high roof, a plus as most drivers can stand up in the van.

The full-sized Ford Transit is the best-selling larger cargo van in the United States and is also rated the most reliable. You can choose from 3 engine sizes and 3 lengths. The high roof EL version can carry up to 487 cubic feet of cargo!

Because the Ford Transit is so popular, used vans are plentiful in most areas. A five-year-old van with 50,000 miles (most vans can go 250,000 miles or more with no major issues when well maintained.) is just half the price of a new van.

The Ram Promaster is an affordable full-size cargo van, with prices starting about 10% lower than the Ford or Nissan. A generous cargo capacity of up to 460 cubic feet and lots of doors make it easy to access cargo. The front wheel drive makes this van better suited to winter driving than rear wheel drive vans. The optional diesel engine makes sense for long-term durability and fuel economy.

As you can see, there are plenty of solid choices for cargo vans, new or used, and a wide variety of cargo capacities so you can get the size that's best for your courier business routes.

To get a better idea of pricing for used cargo vans, try auto.com, commercialtrucktrader.com, truecar.com and carfax.com (my favorite).

How to Make Your Cargo Van Last 300,000 Miles

It's not uncommon for a well-maintained van to last 250,000 to 300,000 miles, even in commercial use. Here are a few tips to help you get the longest service life for your courier van without spending a lot on expensive and unnecessary repairs.

1. Pay extra for synthetic motor oil when you have your oil changed. Although the cost of synthetic oil is higher, in can extend the life of your engine with better lubrication of moving parts.

    When you're having the oil and oil filter changed, have the coolant, power steering and brake fluids checked.

2. Replace the transmission fluid and filter every 50,000 miles. Most owner's manuals specify 100,000 miles before this service, but everyday stop-and-go commercial service is hard on transmissions. True, it can cost quite a bit, but nothing like the cost of a transmission rebuild.

3. The salt used in many states to melt ice and snow off roads is very corrosive to the underside of your vehicle, so always get an underbody wash when you visit the car wash after a snow or ice storm. Of course, you will have to wait until temperatures are above freezing to have this done.

4. Find a good mechanic who can help you spot many problems before they can do serious damage. Instead of taking your vehicle to a quick oil change shop, have your mechanic do it. This gives them frequent opportunities to do a thorough once-over of your vehicle, including brakes, hoses and belts.

If you don't have a mechanic, go to ASE.com and check on "find a repair shop." Mechanics that are ASE certified have extensive training and are among the best in the business. You can also check AAA.com and search for "approved auto repair."

DAY 26

Success Tips

To succeed with your new courier business, there are four qualities that are essential. Without exception, all successful business owners have these qualities, and you must as well.

Willingness to work - You'll never get ahead in this business unless you are willing to work as hard as it takes to succeed. This can mean long days, but the rewards are worth it.

Persistence - If you get up each time you stumble and keep moving forward, you will succeed. Don't let problems or the occasional difficult customer slow you down or discourage you. Keep focused on your goal of a successful, profitable courier business.

Marketing ability - If you think just being a capable courier is enough, think again. Marketing is not complicated, but it means you continually must let others know about your business and give them a reason to hire you the first time. We've covered lots of free and low cost marketing methods in earlier chapters.

While you can expect happy customers to provide plenty of referrals, you still need to sell yourself to prospects and other sources of referrals to keep busy and profitable. Fortunately, there are several free and low-cost ways to do that, which we explored in earlier chapters.

Service - The courier business is a service business, and if you don't provide good service, your business will struggle. Service is all about the small touches, like making sure the flowers you deliver arrive in perfect condition, or making a rush delivery for a special customer outside your normal business hours. If you provide good service, you will never have to worry about the competition.

Ten Courier Success Tips

1. To gain experience and skills, consider working for an established courier service business, either as an employee or as an independent contractor. You'll find a list in the Resource chapter.

2. Build customer confidence by dressing and acting like a pro. Wearing a polo shirt and cap with your company name or logo is an inexpensive way to look professional. Your customers will be more likely to have confidence in you if you are neatly dressed and friendly. Don't forget to smile!

3. Always ask your customers if the items they are shipping are hazardous, perishable, fragile or valuable. Most couriers add a surcharge to shipments that require extra security or paper-work, such as hazardous medical specimens or expensive art-work.

4. Never sign a long-term contract with a customer until you've done at least a two-week test to make sure it's workable (and profitable) for you.

5. Be sure to get the customer to sign and print their name so there will be no confusion about who signed for a delivery. You'll be amazed at how illegible some signatures can be.

6. Use a separate delivery log sheet for each customer so you can mail copies of the log sheet along with an invoice at the end of the month. This can prevent problems, as the customer can see exactly what they are being billed for.

7. Check in with your regular customers once a month and ask, *"How am I doing?"* This regular feedback will help you address any specific issues and ensure that your customers remain happy and loyal to you.

8. Don't forget to ask those happy customers for referrals, either in person or with a simple postcard.

9. Build a "time cushion" into your driving schedule. This helps when, for example, a customer doesn't have a package ready when you arrive to pick it up, or you get stuck in traffic.

10. Visit one new prospect every business day to plant the seeds for future business. Leave a printed notepad and your business card. Every time they make a note, your business name is right there!

Why You Should Love Complaints

Complaints can be a powerful marketing tool if you encourage them and handle them well. Once a month, check in with your regular customers to ask them how you're doing. Ask if they are happy with your service. Could it be improved? Any services they would like to see added?

When you do this, you might get complaints—some mild and some not so mild. That's okay. You want customers to complain, and here's why:

- ✓ Unhappy customers tell others about you. That won't happen if you listen and correct any problems.
- ✓ If your customers don't complain, you'll never know of any problems and won't be able to fix them.
- ✓ If one customer is having a problem, others could too.
- ✓ Even if customers don't complain, when they are unhappy with your service, they are likely to switch to your competition.

Here's a simple four-step method for turning complaints into happy customers:

1. **Say "I'm sorry."** These two powerful words can calm an angry customer and let them know you accept responsibility.

2. **Find a solution.** First, let them talk to be sure you understand the reason they have a complaint. After you are sure you "get it", do what is necessary to resolve the problem quickly.

3. **Thank your customer.** Let them know you appreciate bringing the problem to your attention and ask them to let you know the next time there is a problem.

4. **Follow up.** After you have solved the problem that prompted the customer's complaint, follow up in person, if possible, to let them know what you did for them, and ask if that is acceptable for them.

DAY 27

Just Go Network!

Networking is the most effective way to build your courier business. It cost almost nothing - just your time. It's about building relationships with others with the goal of mutual benefit. It's more than passing out business cards. Networking is a two-way street, not just about trying to get something out of someone.

Networking is also about building trust. People always prefer to buy a product or service from someone they know, like and trust. Think about it. Would you rather let a stranger deliver your packages or get it done by someone recommended by a friend or business associate?

Yet, if you're shy like me and so many others, just the thought of networking can be intimidating. When networking, remember you are building relationships, not make a sale. Here are a few proven tips to get you started:

1. Be genuine. Don't try to be someone else. If you're not a natural extrovert, that's perfectly okay.

2. Networking is about making friends. If you've ever made friends, you know how to network.

3. No one cares about you. All they care about is themselves. That's why you need to give something to other people you meet, whether

they're potential customers or fellow couriers, without expecting them to do something in return.

4. When you give something to others, it creates an unspoken, often subconscious, need to return the favor. That's why networking works so well.

5. "You can have everything in life you want if you will just help other people get what they want." Zig Ziglar

6. Be visible. Networking is a contact sport and the more people you contact and become visible to, the more you will build your business through networking.

7. When you're talking with someone, listen more than you speak. Give them your full attention and make them feel important by listening to them. When you do that, they will trust, like and respect you.

8. In your conversations with others, practice your ABCs (Always Be Curious). Ask what they do, ask about their family, what they do for fun.

9. Just do it - start a conversation with someone you haven't met yet and don't forget your ABCs.

Networking is an easy way to gain exposure for your courier business in the community. Groups such as the Chamber of Commerce, Rotary and Kiwanis, and other business organizations can provide an opportunity to meet, greet, and become better known. Besides groups, spread the word among related businesses, such as dry cleaners, pharmacies and flower shops that don't offer delivery services.

Both national and regional courier associations offer many benefits to your new courier business. You can often get discounted business insurance and special deals on cargo vans and other courier equipment.

In addition, you'll find a network of other couriers that you can turn to. If you have questions, a member can probably answer them.

Here are several regional and national courier associations to check out:

CLDA. Customized Logistics and Delivery Association is a national organization that offers educational programs and events and a regular magazine and newsletters. www.clda.org

New York State Messenger and Courier Association. If you live or work in New York State, you'll have an opportunity to network and learn more about the local industry. wwwnysmca.org

National Ground Delivery Association. If you deliver packages, you'll want to check out this trade group, which offers many resources, services and discounted products to members. www.grounddelivery.org

Florida Messenger Association offers seminars and workshops across Florida and an online directory of members to help businesses find a local courier company. www.floridamessenger.org

Association for Delivery Drivers offers a variety of tools to members, workshops and training programs. www.a4dd.org

California Delivery Association. Lots of resources and deals for courier s in the golden state. www.cadelivery.org

National Home Delivery Association. Specialized focus on the "white glove" delivery of appliances, electronics and furniture to homes. www.nationalhomedeliveryassociation.com

Massachusetts Delivery Association. Independent contractor couriers and messengers within the state. www.madeliveryassociation.com

Texas Courier and Logistics Association. A Facebook group helping Texas-based couriers. www.Facebook.com/pg/texascourierlogisticsassoc

Networking with Future Customers

Providing a list of services you offer will help generate calls and jobs. Don't worry about being too specific with your list. Just cover the general services you plan to offer and add a line at the end, such as *"Don't see what you're looking for? Call us to discuss your needs."*

DEPENDABLE COURIER SERVICE

What: Documents and any package that will fit in a van.

When: We are ready to go when you call.

How Far: Most of our deliveries are within 50 miles of Anytown, but we can deliver anywhere.

SERVICE OPTIONS

Regular: Pickup and delivery in 4 hours.

Rush: Pickup and delivery in 2 hours.

Stat: Pickup and delivery in 1 hour.

Economy: pickup and delivery within 24 hours.

What we deliver: Art, documents, dry cleaning, flowers, food, medical specimens, plans, product delivery, prescriptions.

"Don't see what you're looking for? Call us to discuss your needs."

To determine what services are needed in your area, visit or call potential customers. Tell them you plan to start a courier service and want to find out what services they may need.

Here is a short list of questions to ask that will help you determine the best services to offer:

- ✓ Are you using a courier/errand service now?
- ✓ If yes, which service do you use, and are you happy with them? Do they offer all the courier services you want?
- ✓ How frequently do you use or need courier service?
- ✓ How quickly do you need deliveries completed?
- ✓ What courier services would you like to see available?

Don't sell your service. This is just an information gathering visit. It also allows you to get acquainted with potential future customers, so a future visit to sell your services will be easier. If you're visiting a larger company, ask who is the best person to contact about courier services.

DAY 28

Time to Grow - Adding Employees

Whether you plan to hire new employees now or in the future, it's important to do it right. Because of the complexities of today's labor laws, federal and state regulations and record-keeping involved, you need to know of these requirements before you even place your first help wanted ad.

Hiring the best people for your new courier business will free you to focus on the "big picture" that will help you grow your business, give you a backup person who can take over a route when you are sick or on vacation and increase your profits as you add new customers.

After you have hired and trained your new employee, you will also gain precious time to keep learning more about your new courier business with workshops and seminars. You'll also gain the time to build your network of prospects and other courier businesses, which will help your business to grow.

As your business grows, you will gain new customers, but without help, you may have to turn away those new customers because you're already over-extended and over-worked! That's not good. In addition, with good help, you will serve your existing customers better.

When is it time to hire employees?

1. Do you feel you just can't ever take a day off? Without employees, you can forget vacations or sick days. Just one employee can give you the personal time you need and deserve.

2. Are you turning down new customers? When you have to say "no" to new customers or work longer hours just to keep up, it's time to get the help that will allow you to expand your business and become more profitable.

3. Are your customers unhappy? When your customers complain about poor service, late deliveries or service that's bad for business. It's a sign that you need to add an employee so you can spend more time keeping your customers happy. As I mentioned in an earlier chapter, the customer signs your paycheck.

4. Do you feel overwhelmed by your workload? Do you look forward to your work every day, or do you dread it? When you're stressed or unhappy about your work, it shows, and your customers will sense it. When you love your work, it shows, and a smile on your face sends a huge positive signal to your customers.

5. Do you have a life outside your work? When you neglect your personal life because you're working all the time, guess who suffers? Your family and friends. If this describes you, it may be time to add and employee and get your "real" life back!

6. You want to grow your business, but you never seem to have time to pursue new opportunities or plan your business future. Hiring an employee can give you that vital time to plan for your bigger and better courier business.

If you found yourself saying "yes" to one or more of these six reasons, read on while we cover the right way to find and hire your first new employee.

DAY 29

Finding Good Employees

Start with a job description. To attract the right applicants, you need to write a simple job description. Focus on education, experience and "soft skills," such as a "people person" ability to organize and time management.

A good courier can organize their daily deliveries to plan an efficient route that saves time and fuel. If any deliveries are time-sensitive, such as documents or medical specimens, that requires good organizational skills.

A G.E.D. or a high school diploma is a reasonable minimum requirement, as courier work requires the ability to read and write at a basic level. Also, I've found new hires with a recent military background to be excellent employees, as the military service has trained them to be punctual, courteous and eager to succeed in the civilian world.

Older folks in their 50s and 60s can also be capable couriers, especially if your working schedule is flexible. New hires with previous courier or delivery experience can be great hires, and they have proven their ability to do the work with another employer.

Pre - Hiring Setup

Before hiring your first employee, you will need to determine whether you want independent contractors or employees.

The main difference between independent contractors and employees is who is in control of the work, according to the I.R.S. and most states. If a courier is responsible for their own work and scheduling, they could be considered an independent contractor. If they depend on you to supply a list of deliveries, scheduling, and pay, they are considered an employee.

There are a lot of "gray areas" here, and laws vary from state to state, so check with one of the courier organizations listed in the resource chapter for up-to-date information.

Background Checks

A pre-employment background check is recommended for all new hires. Better to get any bad news before you hire than after. What information you can check on depends on your state regulations, but almost all states allow a criminal background check and a drug test, the two most important checks for you to consider.

To order a background check, do a web search for "criminal background check in (your state)" Compare prices from at least 3 providers before you order a check.

The U.S. Equal Employment Opportunity Commission has strict rules that must be followed if you do a background check. You must notify the applicant in writing that you intend to order a background check.

In addition, the applicant must provide a signed consent to the check. If you are ordering a credit check, the same rules apply, plus you must notify the applicant if you refuse to offer the applicant a job because of information in the credit report.

Drug testing is often included in a complete background check, especially because of the nature of courier work. Just imagine for a moment what could happen if a courier employed by you was involved in a serious accident while on their delivery route and was found to be driving under the influence of illegal drugs!

Your insurance company would drop your coverage, those injured could sue you and your business could go bankrupt. So just do it! According to the current federal regulations, an applicant can refuse to take a drug test, but if they do, you probably don't want to hire them, anyway.

The U.S. Civil Rights Act makes it illegal to ask about age, race, ethnicity, color, sex, religion, national origin, disabilities, marital status or pregnancy, whether in a background check, an interview or on a written application.

Advertise Your Job

Once you're prepared, it's time to get the word out. Almost all jobs are listed on online job boards. Explore several to see which one might be the best for your employee search.

Here's a list of the larger national job boards:

    indeed.com

    careerbuilder.com

    Craigslist.org

    linkedin.com

    Monster.com

    glassdoor.com

    simplyhired.com

    seek.com

DAY 30

Employee Record Keeping & Taxes

Insure your new employees. When you hire employees, you must add worker's compensation insurance. This insurance is required in all states and covers injury or illness while on the job.

For an example, if you hired a new delivery driver who injured their back lifting a heavy package, worker's compensation insurance pays for their medical care and wages while they are unable to work.

In most states, worker's compensation insurance is available through private insurance companies. Only four states, Ohio, North Dakota, Washington and Wyoming, have their own state-run insurance plans.

If you're in one of the other 46 states, contact your current insurance agent or insurance broker to set up this insurance. Your agent can also add a new employee to your surety bond.

Why Hire A Bookkeeper?

When you add employees, the quantity and complexity of record-keeping can be overwhelming. Don't make the mistake of trying to do everything yourself. Your focus should be on running and growing your courier business.

Few small business owners have the in-depth knowledge of accounts receivable, accounts payable and taxes, and the yearly changes in tax laws and regulations. It's better to hire a professional who has the training and skills to handle this part of your business.

It's also a form of insurance, as missing a bill or a tax filing could affect your business credit rating or result in substantial fees or tax penalties from your state or the I.R.S.

Be sure to hire a bookkeeper that can handle both taxes and payroll so they can handle estimated tax payments, 1099s for independent contractors, Form 940 employment tax forms, W-2 forms and give you a schedule of what is due and when. Unless you enjoy handling these details daily, do yourself a favor and hire a pro!

Never forget, your time is money that can be used towards running your new courier business and taking it to the next level. A good bookkeeper can save you money by ensuring that you don't make costly accounting mistakes, forget to file a form or a tax payment or forget to send reminders when a customer forgets to pay their bill on time.

If you are on a tight budget, you can use one of the bookkeeping software programs covered in Day 6 to handle the more routine tasks, then transfer the data to a pro for the rest. Quicken, for example, is widely used by bookkeepers and accountants, so sharing date with your bookkeeper is almost seamless.

Save On Taxes

Taxes. Be sure to keep track of all your business-related expenses, as they may be deductible at tax time. Top deductions include:

- ✓ **Vehicle expenses.** At the current 55 cents per mile, this is a huge deduction for most couriers. For many, the mileage deduction alone will cover the cost of a new fuel-efficient vehicle in a year or two.

- ✓ **Startup expenses.** The cost of getting your courier business started is usually deductible. Check with a tax guide or tax professional to get specific deductions.

- ✓ **Education expenses.** If you take classes or workshops to maintain or improve your job skills, they may be deductible. Another good reason for attending the courier convention in Las Vegas next January!

- ✓ **Professional fees.** Fees paid to accountants, tax professionals, lawyers, or other professional consultants are deductible.

- ✓ **Equipment.** Check with a tax pro to see if there are any special "stimulus" deductions available for the purchase of capital equipment such as vehicles and computers.

- ✓ **Interest.** If you use credit to finance business purchases, the interest is deductible.

- ✓ **Advertising.** Any marketing costs, such as a yellow pages ad, a magnetic sign for your vehicle or promotional costs, such as sponsoring a little league team or buying equipment for them, is deductible.

An excellent book on the subject is *Deduct It—Lower Your Small Business Taxes,* available at www.nolo.com.

What To Pay Your Employees

To find good employees, you will need to pay competitive wages. If courier and delivery drivers in your area are making $18 an hour, you need to match that, or finding the best employees will be difficult.

To get started, go to the help-wanted job boards listed earlier and note hourly wages for a courier or delivery drivers in your town. Jot down 10 posted rates, then divide by 10 and you've got the magic number you need to match.

While you're checking the job boards, also study the job descriptions. This will help you write an effective ad or post at the job boards. Some job boards, like Indeed, have a template you can use by simple filling in the blanks for important items like job title, start date, pay rate and required background checks.

Resources

Glossary of Courier Terms

Bill of Lading. The document that describes the details of a shipment, including: shipper, consignee, product description, value and weight.

Blanket wrapping. Special care, typically using mover's blankets, to protect fragile items such as office machines, furniture or appliances.

C.O.D. Means collect on delivery. The courier collects payment from the consignee on delivery.

Consignee. The party to whom a shipment is addressed by the shipper.

Contract carrier. The company that transports freight under contract with a shipper.

CWT. Hundredweight. A hundredweight is equal to 100 pounds.

Dead-heading. Operating a truck without cargo. Common when a trucker delivers a shipment, but does not pick up another load for the return trip.

Declared value. The value of goods declared by the shipper for either shipping charges or carrier liability.

DIM. Dimensional weight, or the space/volume of a shipment. To find the DIM, multiply the length by the width by the height and divide that number by 194.

Hazardous materials. Any materials that are regulated by the U.S. Department of Transportation because they can pose a risk to health, safety or property. Examples are flammable liquids, fertilizers, batteries, infectious substances, toxic compounds, liquids or gases, bleach, perfume or alcohol.

JIT or Just-In-Time. A manufacturing system that depends on small, frequent deliveries of parts and supplies to reduce on-site inventory. In areas with many manufacturers, the JIT system creates a lot of steady work for local courier/delivery companies.

Logbook. The U.S. Department of Transportation requires interstate truckers to keep a logbook to track hours of work for every 24-hour period.

OS&D. Over, short and damaged. A report showing any exceptions on a shipment when it is received by a carrier or consignee.

POD. Proof of delivery.

Prepaid. The shipper is responsible for delivery charges.

White Glove Delivery. Home delivery and light assembly of items delivered (a BBQ, for example) and removal of all packing materials.

How to Add Tracking and Proof-Of-Delivery Using Just Your Smartphone

Tracking and Proof-Of-Delivery is important to your courier service.

Good technology and clean, professional documentation is a direct reflection on your company. It's important to be professional and show potential clients that you are not only reliable and timely but also have state-of-the-art technology. (Don't worry because it's inexpensive and easy to use.)

Something as simple as having professional documentation and being able to track the delivery is a competitive edge. Being able to present your client with a Proof-Of-Delivery (POD) document containing paperwork, signatures, photographs, and time / stamp / location-stamps, makes it easy for both you and your client to see and save information on the delivery.

Having the ability to include photographs in the POD reduces delivery disputes. We have also found that having the ability to include photographs allows couriers to include third-party documentation. For example, you get to a destination and someone has a document for you to include, all you need to do is take a photo, and it will be included in the POD.

As you would expect, having the documentation on the POD eliminates lost or ruined paperwork. It also saves trees because there is less printing of paperwork. Usually, there's no need to purchase hardware. Most people already carry an Apple iPhone, iPad, or Android phone or device. The apps work on IOS (Apple) and Android devices.

Tracking and POD technology is designed to be intuitive and simple to use. The app is understandable and has a high acceptance among couriers and delivery people. Often users of tracking and POD technology have little technical experience but pick it right up.

Being able to immediately know when a pickup and delivery is made adds tremendous efficiency to your business. No more waiting for a call or text that a delivery was completed. The dispatcher will immediately know the courier has completed the delivery and is available for more work. This adds productivity to both dispatching and delivery persons. Even a one-person courier service can enjoy this technology.

We have seen estimates that a courier using an electronic POD app can handle anywhere from 10 to 15% more deliveries per day. Tracking and POD is an obvious, inexpensive and easy way to increase the productivity of your business.

Get started today by visiting deliverymark.com to discover more about this easy-to-use productivity and profit booster.

Forms

You will find two forms on the following pages: a delivery request form and a delivery log form. Add your company information at the top. The forms have not been reviewed by an attorney and are meant as a guide only. You should also have either a self-stick note pad or a door hangar for those deliveries you could not make because no one was there to sign for the delivery. Here's what you want to say:

SORRY WE MISSED YOU

We could not deliver a package from:

Date

Time:

Please call us to make delivery arrangements.

333-255-1234

Delivery Log

Driver_____

Customer_____

Date	Delivery Address	# Items	Signature	Printed Name

Customer Service Request

Date:_____ Customer:_____

Name:_____

Contact Person:_____

Phone: _____

Service: ❏ Pickup ❏ Delivery ❏ Other

        Ready Now ❏ Ready Date & Time:

_____

Delivery / Pick Up Information

Contact Person: _____ Phone: _____

Company Name: _____

Address: _____

Pick up & Delivery Hours: _____

Delivery Deadline: _____

Number of pieces:_____Weight: _____

Type of Service: ❏ Regular ❏ Rush ❏ Stat ❏ Economy

Special Instructions: _____

_____

_____

_____

Payment: ❑ On Customer Account ❑ Credit Card

❑Visa ❑ Mastercard ❑ Amex. Card #_____

Name on card: _____ Expiration Date: _____

Signature: _____

Courier comments: _____

Date completed: _____

Courier Organizations

CLDA. Customized Logistics and Delivery Association is a national organization that offers educational programs and events and a regular magazine and newsletters. www.clda.org

New York State Messenger and Courier Association. If you live or work in New York State, you'll have an opportunity to network and learn more about the local industry. wwwnysmca.org

National Ground Delivery Association. If you deliver packages, you'll want to check out this trade group, which offers many resources, services and discounted products to members. www.grounddelivery.org

Florida Messenger Association offers seminars and workshops across Florida and an online directory of members to help businesses find a local courier company. www.floridamessenger.org

Association for Delivery Drivers offers a variety of tools to members, workshops and training programs. www.a4dd.org

California Delivery Association. Lots of resources and deals for courier s in the golden state. www.cadelivery.org

National Home Delivery Association. Specialized focus on the "white glove" delivery of appliances, electronics and furniture to homes. www.nationalhomedeliveryassociation.com

Massachusetts Delivery Association. Independent contractor couriers and messengers within the state. www.madeliveryassociation.com

Texas Courier and Logistics Association. A Facebook group helping Texas-based couriers. www.Facebook.com/pg/texascourierlogisticsassoc

Messenger Courier Association of the Americas is a non-profit industry association for the messenger courier industry. mcaa.com

The "Gig Economy"—A New Way to Make Money as a Local Courier

Not long ago, musicians were the only people who worked a "gig." Today, there are millions of Americans working gigs instead of having a full-time job.

It started with online marketplaces like Elance and Odesk, where workers could choose short-term work projects that matched their skills. Then along came Etsy, where millions of "makers" create hand-crafted clothing, jewelry and art. Airbnb and other online lodging marketplaces are giving hotels and motels some serious competition by helping individuals around the world provide a place for guests to stay for a night or several months.

Now, Amazon has announced a new gig-style, delivery service that has just launched in Seattle, and will expand soon to other large cities, like New York and Chicago, and eventually to the entire country. It's likely they will offer the program in all other countries where Amazon sells goods.

Amazon is offering to pay its drivers $18 to $24 an hour to deliver packages to their "Prime" customers. The program is called Amazon Flex and requires a few essentials of its drivers:

>   Own a vehicle
>
>   Be over 21

- Have a valid driver's license
- Pass a background check
- Own an Android smartphone

Amazon will give approved drivers a "delivery app" for their smart phone. Drivers can choose to work in 2-hour blocks of time, from as short as 2 hours to as long as 12 hours. This is great for part-timers. Let's say you need to pick up your kids at 3 p.m. No problem, as Amazon Flex allows you to choose your own 2-hour blocks of time to fit your schedule.

Need to earn a lot of money fast? Again, no problem. Just sign up for a long shift or more days per week until you meet your financial goal.

Here's how it works: When you start your shift, you pick up the packages at a central location in your area. Then you deliver those packages in nearby areas. The longer your shift, the larger the area you cover.

Until now, starting your own courier service business could be risky at first, when you're building the business, and income can go up and down. But by using Amazon Flex for a portion of your working hours, you can have a more predictable income right off the bat.

It's important to remember that your income as an independent local courier will be considerable higher—about $36 an hour is typical—for delivery jobs you schedule and complete on your own. So think of Amazon Flex as a "backstop" income source that can give you some income security as you build your own courier service business. To learn more, visit: flex.Amazon.com

Amazon is not the only game in town. Here are a few more options that will help you earn an income right away by making deliveries while you are building your own courier business. For most, all you need is a smartphone and a reliable vehicle.

GoShare is a platform that connects couriers and delivery drivers with trucks and vans to people and businesses that need a same day delivery service. They handle payments, provide supplemental cargo insurance and supply customers who need the service. Sign up at Goshare.com.

Deliv.com is a same-day delivery service for local businesses that is currently operating in almost 40 cities. Drivers can earn up to $20 an hour delivering everything from flowers to clothing from local stores.

Postmates.com is a delivery service that specializes in food and take-out meals. The company says drivers can make up to $25 an hour, depending on their location. Visit their website and scroll down to "join the fleet."

Caviar - This food delivery service is not available in all areas, so check their website, trycaviar.com, to see if they are in yours. You can work when you want, and the company claims you can earn up to $25 an hour plus tips.

GrubHub - One of the larger and older food delivery apps that's available in almost all areas. Flexible hours and hourly rates up to $20 plus tips. GrubHub.com.

Doordash.com is a quick delivery service that gets take-out food from restaurants to customers fast. They serve over 300 cities and thousands of restaurants, and drivers can earn an average of $18 an hour.

Roadie is an on-demand package delivery service for mostly same-day deliveries. Pay is up to $60 for local deliveries and up to $650 for long-haul deliveries. Sign up at: roadie.com

Shipt.com offers same day deliveries of groceries and other household essentials. The company claims you can earn up to $22 an hour shopping and delivering groceries. Unlike the ride share companies, your car can be old and funky, and it's okay.

Uship.com is best for those with a larger vehicle, like a cargo van or utility trailer. They specialize in larger, bulkier items such as office equipment, machinery, furniture, cars, motorcycles and boats, but the pay is good and based on competitive bids.

You visit their website to bid on jobs and pay a small commission for each job. Because winning bids and quotes are open for all to see, you can quickly determine how much to bid.

Haulhound.com is a freight expediting company that helps match shippers and truckers, including those with a cargo van. Most loads are local or regional and require a cargo van with a 2-3 pallet load capacity. Many of the jobs require overnight or same-day delivery, so the pay is much higher on a permile basis.

Courierexpress.net is a logistics company based in Georgia, with most of their jobs in the southeast part of the U.S. If you have a cargo van and live in that area, check them out.

Courierbrokers.com provides a national network to help couriers find deliveries in their area. The service is currently free, so you pay no commission for their services.

Usacouriers.com helps shippers find a local courier to deliver packages for them. Sign up to tap into their national network.

Dropoff.com offers delivery services in many major metropolitan areas and hires independent drivers to offer same-day delivery.

Ontrac.com. OnTrac Logistics is a fast-growing company that currently covers 8 western states and provides a more affordable alternative to UPS and Fedex. They are always looking for local delivery drivers.

Help the Environment and Your Profits.

When gas hit $3 a gallon, Green Express, an Atlanta courier service business, switched to Toyota Prius hybrid electric cars.

Atlanta is one of the top 5 cities for traffic congestion, poor air quality and frequent smog alerts. In addition, everyone at Green Express has kids and did not want to contribute to the air pollution that has made Atlanta one of the worst cities for children's asthma.

Gas is one of the largest expenses of a courier business. After switching to electric hybrids, Green Express found that their new fleet used 46% less fuel than their old cars, and averaged 47 miles per gallon.

An additional bonus is that electric hybrid cars are zero-emission vehicles when stuck in traffic or moving below 30 mph. At highway speeds, they put out just one-third the greenhouse gases from conventional gas-powered cars.

Because of becoming a "green courier service business," Green Express has landed dozens of new customers who love helping to keep reduce pollution in Atlanta by supporting a cleaner delivery service.

Green Express also uses GPS navigation in every vehicle to boost efficiency even more by finding alternate routes to avoid traffic congestion.

An unexpected bonus of using the most efficient routes and zero-emission cars—customers now regularly use Green Express to run personal errands also, saving them time, money and reducing pollution even more.

If you plan to start a courier service, think green, as the fuel savings in your first year could go a long way towards paying for a new Prius or other hybrid electric car. To learn more about Green Express, visit their website, http://greendelivers.com

Disclaimer

No part of this book may not be reproduced or transmitted in any form without the written permission of the author. We have tried to make this book complete and accurate. Although the author has prepared this guide with great care and have tried to insure the accuracy of the information, we assume no responsibility or liability for errors, inaccuracies or omissions. All information in this book is for educational purposes only. Before you begin, check with the appropriate authorities to ensure compliance with all laws and regulations. This guide is sold with the understanding that the publisher is not engaged in rendering legal, accounting or other professional services. If professional assistance is needed, you should seek the services of a competent professional.

> *"You've got to believe in the possibilities. You've got to believe that tomorrow can be better than today. And here's the big one. Believe in yourself!"*
>
> — JIM ROHN

Thank You for Reading!

Dear Reader,

First, thank you for purchasing and reading this book. I hope it has provided both the resources and the motivation for you to start your own local courier business. Starting your own small business is the ticket to a better life and a prosperous future, and freedom from worries about job security.

If you have the time, I'd really love a review. Reviews are a huge help to authors, myself included. If you enjoy this book, please take a minute or two to post a review on Amazon. Just enter the title of this book at Amazon.com, then click on "reviews," then "write a review." Thanks so much for your support!

Wishing you much success in your new business,

Craig Wallin

Printed in Great Britain
by Amazon